San Francisco and Beyond

101 Affordable Excursions

Fun, Historic, Cultural
and Outdoors things to do...

All for $6 or less per person!

by Pamela P. Hegarty

Travel for Less Press

On the Cover: Children get up close and personal with dolphins at the California Academy of Sciences' Steinhart Aquarium. See story in For Kids of All Ages chapter.

San Francisco and Beyond: 101 Affordable Excursions

ISBN 0-9630791-1-5

Published by   Travel for Less Press
                      209 Apollo Dr., Suite 5
                      Hercules, CA 94547
                      (510) 741-8440

Printed and Bound in the United States of America

Special Sales: This book is available at special discounts for quantity purchases for promotions or premiums. For more information, contact the publisher.

This book is dedicated to Brian, to my family
and to the enthusiastic volunteers who keep these
wonderful sites affordable for all of us.

Table of Contents

WE GOT CULTURE   61

TOWNS TO EXPLORE   95

LITERARY LANDMARKS   121

Welcome

San Francisco and Beyond is more than a region. It is a bounty of fun activities, fascinating histories, intriguing cultures and unparalleled natural beauty. Best of all, these precious treasures are surprisingly affordable.

In reviewing the hundreds of travel stories I've published on northern California, I discovered that more than two-thirds of them—many of my favorites—actually cost $6 or less per person. More than half are free!

More than a quick listing, here are the in-depth stories behind these top-notch sites. San Francisco and Beyond: 101 Affordable Excursions is a storybook, keepsake and where-to guide all rolled into one. It will entertain you and inspire you to explore facets of California you may never have known existed.

These excursions are organized by "get out and see it" topics, followed by a geographical cross-reference section for easy planning.

You'll go "Behind the Scenes" at a glassblower's studio, a school for sea lions and the world's largest almond factory.

"Kids of All Ages" will climb aboard antique railroads, defy gravity and design a bike on computer.

You will explore cultural enclaves, "Historic Haunts," hidden gardens and much more.

Make a day of it. Many of these excursions take less than two hours. With the spotting maps in the

"Where It's At" cross-reference section, you can plan to visit more than one site in an area, perhaps bring a picnic lunch along.

Even more fun activities are listed in the "Bonus Coupon Section." These coupons offer discounts to many of the area's most popular attractions—both complementing and in addition to the 101 excursions covered in the text.

The trend is clear. More of us are enjoying shorter, activity-filled trips. If you have a free day or weekend, this guide is your key to spur-of-the-moment excursions that are fun, intriguing, exciting, enlightening and, best of all, surprisingly affordable!

👁 *Levi Strauss Factory*

It carries America's oldest apparel trademark. It was declared an essential commodity by the U.S. government during World War II. It's been enshrined in the Smithsonian. It's been worn by toddlers, teenagers and presidents. Today, it's sold in more than 70 countries.

It is none other than Levi's denim jean. You can learn the history of this American fashion icon and see how they are stitched together in San Francisco at the oldest functioning Levi's factory in the world..

The man behind these world-renowned pants is German-born Levi Strauss. In 1853, his brother-in-law, sensing opportunity in San Francisco during the booming gold rush years, convinced Strauss to join him here and start a dry goods business.

Strauss brought his goods with him, but sold most of his stock to his shipmates on the 17,000-mile voyage from New York around Cape Horn. On arrival, he still had a supply of canvas for tents and Conestoga wagon covers.

Like any good salesman, Strauss soon discovered that what his clients, the miners, really wanted were heavy, sturdy pants that wouldn't wear out in the diggings. Tent canvas was swiftly transformed to what Strauss called "waist-high overalls." He never liked the term "jeans," a word derived from the cotton trousers worn by sailors from Genoa, Italy.

The miners loved them. Strauss quickly exhausted his supply of canvas. He switched to a sturdy fabric called serge from Nimes, France, or "serge de Nimes," eventually shortened to "denim." When miners complained that the weight of gold nuggets ripped their pockets, Strauss worked with a Carson City tailor to add rivets to stress points. In 1873, they patented the innovation.

If you're wondering where the name "501" for today's original shrink-to-fit, button-fly Levi's came from, it was the initial catalog number in the 1890s. Over the last century, the Levi's 501 design has become an American classic.

The factory tour begins with a 1/2-hour documentary made by British television on the Levi's mystique. Not just a durable working pant, Levi's came to represent the ideals of the rugged west and, in the 1950s and '60s, the uniform of the counterculture.

A small museum contains historic photos, a copy of Strauss' patent, a pair of brown duck pants from the turn of the century, original 501 jeans from the 1930s and other styles of Levi's clothing through the years.

Upstairs, you can peek into the styling department where designs for next season are created. This room is devoted to the Brittania line.

You also look in on Levi's laboratories. One is devoted to product evaluation. You may see an employee tugging and inspecting new materials to see if their quality matches Levi's needs. The second research laboratory, with its bottles of colored liquids, is where innovative treatments are concocted, such as the trendy stonewashed jeans.

Downstairs, you can walk past rows of workers piecing blue jeans together. Some sew just the pockets, others press open seams or punch in rivets, still others inspect the finished pants. By the time you finish your tour of Levi Strauss, you'll have a new appreciation for your old blue jeans.

Tours are arranged for groups only, but individuals can hook up with a group tour by calling a day ahead. Allow about 1 1/2 hours for the tour.

Levi Strauss Factory Tour
Valencia at 14th Sts., San Francisco
415/565-9159
Tours Wed. 10:30 & 1
Free

☞ *Walking Tours of San Francisco*

Did you know that San Francisco's financial section is built on hundreds of sunken ships abandoned by gold-seekers? That Robert Louis Stevenson wrote a goodly part of <u>Treasure Island</u> and <u>Kidnapped</u> in Portsmouth Square? That Mark Twain met the original Tom Sawyer where the Transamerica Pyramid now stands?

You'll learn these fun facts about San Francisco and much more on the free Friends of the Library City Guides walking tours. This is certainly one of the city's best bargains, led by enthusiastic guides who know and love San Francisco as well as anyone. Eighteen different tours are offered, including City Hall, Haight/Ashbury, Pacific Heights Mansions and Historic Market Street, plus special neighborhood tours in May and October.

The financial section isn't exactly on the top of the typical tourist's list, but the Gold Rush City walk sheds new light on the fascinating history of the area. The group meets in front of the Transamerica pyramid on the corner of Montgomery and Clay, an appropriate location to begin a talk about how San Francisco burst into a major metropolis.

In 1848, Montgomery Street was the shoreline of a sleepy mission town called Yerba Buena. Clay Street was a pier, when suddenly—Gold! The discovery in the Sierra sparked a rush like none ever seen. By 1850, California's population exploded from 10,000 to more than 100,000 men and several hundred women.

Sailing ships deluged the harbor, but captains and crews deserted them to head for the golden mountain. Some masts were torn down and used as tent poles. Other ships became laundries, hotels and brothels. Eventually, the remains of about 400 ships were scuttled and used as landfill, along with garbage and sand, for the growing city.

A rooming house once stood on the Transamerica pyramid site. Some of the renowned guests include writers Mark Twain, Robert Louis Stevenson and Bret Harte. Twain met a fireman in the public baths downstairs whose name he took a fancy to—Tom Sawyer.

A walk across the street reveals often-overlooked plaques celebrating the Pony Express. During the Express' short heyday, riders carried the mail as far west as Sacramento, where it was ferried by ship to Clay Street pier.

Robert Louis Stevenson enjoyed spending time in nearby Portsmouth Square, now the heart of Chinatown. From a bench here, he could look out and see the many sailing ship masts that inspired Treasure Island and Kidnapped. Today, a monument commemorates the site.

The group heads north on Montgomery to see some of the finest examples of San Francisco's earliest streets. Two brick buildings constructed during the gold rush were some of the few that survived the 1906 quake, but had to be abandoned after the 1989 quake.

Gold Street is one of the few remaining narrow, originally waterfront alleys. It's connected to Jackson Street by short Balance Street, whose name is from the ship, Balance, upon which it was built.

Gold Rush City is just one of 18 different tours offered year-round. Some meet on weekdays. Most are scheduled on weekends. For a schedule of tours, send a self-addressed, stamped envelope to the address below or call to hear a recording of upcoming tours. Expect to spend about 1 1/2 hours for each walk.

City Guides, Friends of the Library
Main Library, Civic Center, San Francisco 94102
415/557-4266
Generally, tours scheduled Tu.-Th. Noon;
Sat. & Sun.at various times
Free

👁 *Acres of Orchids*

From happy, golden "dancing dolls" to bridal white "snowdrift," orchids are the largest and arguably the most beautiful flowering groups in the plant kingdom.

About 30,000 species and more than 1,000,000 hybrids of orchids flourish in every country in the world except the polar regions. Thousands of new varieties have been created at Rod McLellan's Acres of Orchids in South San Francisco, the world's largest orchid hybridizer.

Neophyte gardeners and orchid aficionados alike shouldn't miss the Acres of Orchids tours held at 10:30 and 1:30 daily. You can see how these intricate flowers are cultivated, enjoy the colorful variety of blooms in their retail greenhouse and take a favorite home with complete instructions on care and feeding.

Plan to spend about an hour for this look into the horticulture of orchids and the history of the McLellan family in California's floral industry.

The family business began back in 1859 when Rod McLellan's grandfather, David, came west with his new bride to explore the gold country. They soon discovered that panning for gold wasn't the road to riches. Instead, they started growing vegetables and sold them to prospectors.

The love of growing was passed through the generations. David's son, Edgar, delved particularly into flowers. He realized the enormous potential in the San Francisco area's fine growing climate and the high demand for flowers back East. The McLellan family was instrumental in developing the state's air freight industry and new packaging methods in the shipment of perishable products.

One popular item was the gardenia corsage, which was invented here. On the tour, you can watch workers carefully assemble and package these delicate, sweet-smelling corsages for shipment around the country.

Greenhouses cover a good part of McLellan's 35 acres of land in South San Francisco, the base of operations which also handles products from a 112-acre Watsonville farm.

Although they grow gardenias, roses, eucalyptus and a variety of cut flowers, they are best known for their orchids, thanks to the third generation of McLellans, Rod, known as "the orchid grower's orchid grower."

The tour winds through the maze of greenhouses where orchids are hybridized, cultivated and repotted. One greenhouse is "the nursery in the nursery."

The plants begin with a fine, powdery substance, the tiniest seed in the world. The seeds are placed in a jar with a gel-like mixture of water, sugar and agar, which is powdered seaweed.

Acres of Orchids also uses a cloning process to reproduce orchids, but either way, the cultivator must be meticulous and patient. In a sterile lab, specialists in white coats use a tweezers to thin tiny leaves half the size of your baby fingernail from one jar to another. It takes eight to ten years before the plant is mature enough to bloom.

Allow time to browse in McLellan's retail greenhouse. Although 80% of their plants are sold wholesale, you can buy one for your home here or through their mail-order catalog. Contrary to popular belief, orchids are not difficult to grow, nor fragile, nor temperamental, according the McLellan's experts. The confusion stems from the wide variety of orchids. Knowledgeable sales people recommend the best plants for your climate and lifestyle. Care and feeding sheets will help ensure that your plant blooms year after year.

Acres of Orchids
1450 El Camino Real, South San Francisco
Open daily 8-5; tours daily 10:30 and 1:30
415/871-5655
Free

👁 *Sunset Magazine*

Did you ever wonder why the recipes in <u>Sunset Magazine</u> taste so good? This behind-the-scenes tour of the magazine's offices reveals the answer. You're invited to look in on their busy kitchen, where every recipe is tested and retested three or more times before finding its way onto the pages of <u>Sunset</u>.

The tour begins in the main office building, which feels more like a home than corporate headquarters. If not for the reception desk in the lobby, you'd think you were entering someone's livingroom. Even the reception desk is tasteful—a carved wood antique from 15th-century Italy.

Picture windows frame <u>Sunset's</u> famous gardens. Comfortable sofas invite you to relax and browse over <u>Sunset</u> books and magazines. They are displayed proudly but unobtrusively on the bookshelves and coffee tables.

Finely woven Native American blankets warm the desert tile floor. Western paintings, including the 1884 "Among the Giant Redwoods," by renowned landscape artist Thomas Hill, and a portrait of <u>Sunset's</u> inspiration, L.W. and Ruth Lane, hang on the walls. <u>Sunset</u> embraces its motto as "the magazine of western living."

<u>Sunset</u> first appeared in May 1898 as a publication of the Southern Pacific Railroad, who designed it to entice settlers to the west. Its name is derived from the *Sunset Limited*, the train that ran from New Orleans to Los Angeles. Its first front cover, displayed as a poster near the lobby, shows one of today's most recognized west coast landmarks, a view of the Golden Gate—but without the bridge.

In 1928, it was bought by the Lane family and became a regional magazine emphasizing gardening, cooking, home improvement and travel. <u>Sunset</u>

Magazine now boasts about 1.4 million subscribers and produces how-to and travel books, instructional videotapes and language workbooks. Although Sunset recently was bought by Time Warner, its goals, editorial direction and working ambience remain the same.

On the tour, you can pick up hints on how to display colorful, healthy plants throughout the year on your patio. Containers brimming with bright blossoms are interspersed throughout Sunset's secluded courtyards.

Inside, the spicy aroma of western cooking entices the tour group to the test kitchen. Visitors can peer through the glass wall as Sunset's eight food editors test their own recipes and recipes sent in by readers.

What happens to all that delicious food? On one counter, plates of prepared recipes are laid out for the lucky employees at Sunset. If the counter displays a green flag, it means the food turned out well. If the flag is black, it means nothing is wrong with the food, but it's not up to Sunset's standards, i.e., eat it but don't comment.

Sunset's gardens are not included on the tour, but you're free to enjoy them at your leisure. The gardens form a semi-circle around Sunset's perfectly trimmed, 18-hole putting green lawn.

The plantings are a mini-version of the west coast from Canada to Mexico, moving from the north coast rhododendrons at one end, through the forests of Monterey to the cactus garden representing Mexico. It's the perfect inspiration to cultivate Sunset's magazines gardening tips into your own landscape.

Sunset Magazine Tour
Corner of Willow and Middlefield Rds.,
Menlo Park
415/324-5479
Mon.-Fri. 10:30 & 2:30
Free

👁 *Long Marine Laboratory*

Can you teach an old dolphin new tricks? What can sea lions learn? How do you become friends with a creature from the ocean world? Students at the UC Santa Cruz Long Marine Laboratory are learning the answers first hand and you're invited for a behind-the-scenes peek at their watery "classroom."

Long Marine Lab is located just beyond Natural Bridges State Park, along the coast north of Santa Cruz. You have to drive off the beaten path past fields of Brussels sprouts to get here, but you'll be rewarded with a compact aquarium, small museum and friendly docents to show you the sequestered tanks of sea lions.

One impressive exhibit is Long's 85-foot blue whale skeleton, one of only two blue whale skeletons in California. The docent will tell you that the blue whale is the largest animal that ever lived—larger even than Tyrannosaurus Rex. This whale washed ashore at nearby Pescadero. The immense skeleton is displayed in the courtyard, dwarfing the lab's small work trailers that encircle it.

Inside the museum is a piece of baleen, the fibrous material through which whales eat. The largest animal eats some of the world's smallest creatures—single-cell plankton—2,000 to 3,000 pounds of it each day. A collection of scrimshaw recalls the era when these extraordinary animals were severely hunted.

The museum is squeezed into a trailer, but it holds several intriguing pieces. The sea otter skeleton reveals a bone structure similar to humans, especially the legs. The otter is one of the only sea animals with fur. Other sea creatures have blubber to keep warm. The otter was hunted almost to extinction for its dense coat, with some 600,000 hairs per square inch of fur.

Long's cozy aquarium focuses on life in nearby waters. Tanks are filled with rose-colored anemones, a slithering eel and camouflaged fish. Kids plunge their hands into the cool water of the touch tank to feel its starfish and anemones and see them close-up.

The most exciting part of Long Marine Lab is behind the high fences, when docents escort you to the students' hands-on classroom. Animals change depending on the research. On the day you visit, you may see a barking sea lion. Those "trained seals" you enjoy in public aquariums are actually sea lions, some of which prepared for the big time here.

The students' first goal, no matter what the animal, is to teach them to become used to humans so they can be hand-inspected periodically for illness. Once comfortable, the animals here seem to truly enjoy the company of the students who clean the pools or conduct studies.

This is a working laboratory, and you may not get to see all the animals close-up if a training experiment is in progress, but a path up the hill above affords an overview of all the lab activities and a unique peek at our friends from the sea.

Long Marine Laboratory
End of Delaware Ave. (along the coast)
Santa Cruz
408/459-2883
Wed.-Sun. 1-4
Free

👁 *Glass Blowers of Benicia*

Frank Sinatra and the Pope may not see eye-to-eye on much, but they do share one thing in common. Both have used the stylish glassware of Yuba Arts, three small, unassuming studios located in the industrial outskirts of Benicia, about an hour's drive east of San Francisco. Sinatra imbibes from Smyers' "red flash" goblet set. Nourot Glass created 2,000 communion bowls for the 1987 Papal Mass in San Francisco.

Nourot Glass was the first studio to move to the Benicia waterfront from San Francisco. It encompasses the talents of three artists, Michael Nourot, Ann Corcoran and David Lindsay. Now, two more studios, Smyers and Zellique, share this off-the-beaten-path location.

During the week, you can visit these three studios, known collectively as Yuba Arts, and watch the artists blow glass blobs into enviable masterpieces. Usually, at least one glassblower is at work on any given weekday from about 10 A.M. to 4 P.M. In their showroom, you can purchase the finished pieces and one-of-a-kind creations or seconds at near wholesale prices.

Although they share the love of glass, blowing technique and a common location, each studio embraces a unique style, distinctive in look and sensation.

Nourot creates perfume bottles and vases of seafoam green, delicate aqua and subtle roses, combined with a swirl of grace that convinced even the master of gracefulness, Rudolf Nureyev, to purchase their pink marble cabinet vase.

Michael Nourot studied at the respected Venini Factory in Italy. He incorporates traditional Italian glass blowing techniques into his contemporary designs. Nourot creations are exhibited in galleries across the United States, in Europe and Japan.

Next door to Nourot is Smyers Glass. Smyers' distinctive glassware has been featured in <u>Bon Appetit</u>, <u>Gourmet</u>, <u>Architectural Digest</u> and <u>Metropolitan Home</u>. Bette Midler, Tina Turner and Richard Dreyfuss are a few of the celebrities who entertain guests with Smyers pitchers and stemware. Their martini set is one that James Bond would covet, with clean, sleek lines highlighted with a free-flowing spiral. Deep greens, rubies and cobalt blues dissolve into clear glass in some pieces. Like all Yuba Arts glass, each is individually handblown.

Zellique Art Glass is the creation of Joseph Morel, who opened his studio in Benicia in 1980. He has spent more than 15 years perfecting his craft, but still enthusiastically describes the transformation of glass into a stylish bowl as "magic."

One of his most popular creations is a plump love bird paperweight complete with inner heart. Other popular pieces are the crystal heart perfume bottles and seascape series paperweights. Zellique glass is sold in many galleries, museums and gift shops as well as such upscale department stores as Nieman-Marcus and Nordstroms.

After you visit the studios, stop by the showroom to see the stunning finished products. Some pieces are seconds. They sell for as little as a third of retail. They aren't defective, but have some cosmetic fault, such as a small bubble in the glass. Some may be slightly larger or smaller than standard. You also can find perfectly made prototypes, one-of-a-kind experiments that aren't sold to retailers. It's an excellent place to find a unique gift or begin your collection of art glass.

Yuba Arts Glass Studios
East end of H St., near 6th St., Benicia
Nourot 707/745-1463
Smyers 707/745-2614
Zellique 707/745-5710
Mon.-Fri. 10-4
Free

☜ *California Cooperative Creamery*

Do you know someone crazy about cows? Then you'll find that perfect gift at The Creamery Store in Petaluma. Herded into one compact boutique are more than 600 items inspired by the distinctive black and white markings of California's dairy cows, from candlesticks to soap dispensers, cocktail napkins to boxer shorts.

The gift shop is a spin-off from one of the area's leading businesses—the California Cooperative Creamery. The cooperative's dairies produce more than one million gallons of milk every day. On the creamery's behind-the-scenes tour, you can see how that milk is made into our state's favorite cheeses.

A 15-minute video illustrates the cooperative's history and the massive inner workings of the creamery. It all began in 1913 with 33 Sonoma and Marin County dairies. Their 1,900 cows yielded about 6,650 gallons of milk each day, which was bought to the fledgling cooperative in horse-drawn wagons. Most of the milk was churned into butter for the San Francisco market.

Today, you'll see immense, two-tank stainless steel trucks bringing the milk from the dairy to the creamery. At last count, their 540-plus dairies milked more than 125,000 cows twice a day. The guide will lead you back into the working creamery. You can watch through a window as ultra-modern machinery transforms 5,000 gallons of milk at a time into one batch of your favorite Monterey Jack or Cheddar.

Everything is shiny stainless steel, from the heating tanks to the mixing tables. After the milk is heat pasteurized, a secret starter culture is added.

Only the creamery's master cheesemakers know its precise ingredients. The milk is then heated in large tanks until, at a certain temperature, it becomes curds and whey.

Most of the whey, which is liquid protein, is sent back to the dairies to feed the cows. The curds, more the consistency of scrambled eggs, are pumped onto long, 5,000-gallon mixing tables where the remaining whey is drained off. Pailfuls of salt and hot peppers, for hot pepper jack, are added by hand.

The cheese is then vacuumed off the table and sent into two-story-high chutes where it is fashioned into huge blocks. These blocks are sold wholesale or cut and packaged into the familiar random-size portions we buy in our local supermarket. All together, the process from milk to a block of cheese takes about six hours.

Back at the gift shop, you can taste free samples of the freshly made cheese, buy your favorite brands to enjoy at home and order gift boxes to be sent to those on your gift list along with, perhaps, a pair of black and white diary cow boxer shorts.

California Cooperative Creamery
711 Western Avenue, Petaluma
· 707/778-1234
Store open Mon.-Sat. 10-5
Tours Mon.-Sat. 11-3, starting every hour
Free

Extra Tip...Did you know that cheddar cheese, like fine wine, is aged? Cheddars are aged in large refrigerated warehouses kept between 35° to 40°. Mild cheddar is aged about 30 days, Medium four to six months. Sharp is aged about nine months and Extra Sharp for one year. Monterey Jack, on the other hand, usually is best eaten within 120 days. Generally, Monterey Jack gets bitter with age. Cheddar gets better. But your palate is your best guide.

☜👁 *Oldest Working Oyster Farm*

Raw or barbecued, delicate cocktails or mammoth "cowboys," they don't come any fresher than the Tomales Bay Oyster Company. Located five miles north of Point Reyes Station on Highway 1 (check your odometer and look for the sign on the left), you will find a unique eating experience here. The manager will be glad to show you how these sought-after specialties are grown and harvested.

Begun in 1909, Tomales Bay Oyster Company is the oldest working oyster farm in California. The company's founder, Oscar Johanson, who recently celebrated his 100th birthday, still drops in occasionally to sample the goods. Maybe there is something to the health mystique of oysters. They are high in protein, calcium and other minerals and have zero fat. Even the ancient Greeks and Romans relished the oyster's unique benefits.

Unlike other industries, high tech hasn't found its way into oystering. All you will see here are a few weathered buildings, the retail oyster tanks, a pier piled with oyster-growing and sorting boxes and several small boats. But don't let the three-person operation fool you. In the shallow waters beyond the pier are nearly two million oysters.

Environmental factors don't allow oysters to reproduce in these waters, so baby oysters, about the size of a fingernail, must be shipped in from a Eureka lab. They are seeded into wire mesh "bags," then planted in the shallow waters.

After four months, they have grown to about 1/2" to 1" long, but do not have much depth, or meat, to them. They are removed from the water and separated into additional bags to give them more room to grow. After one year, they are ready to be sold as the popular cocktail-sized oysters.

Harvesting, like everything else at Tomales Bay, is done the old-fashioned way—by hand. At low tide, be it noon or midnight, the harvester pulls on his thigh-high waders, ties a small rowboat to his waist and pushes his way through the knee-deep mud. He will fill and empty his boat three or four times before the day's harvest is complete.

The color of the oyster varies according to the type and color of organisms the oyster has ingested. Oysters filter eight gallons of water every hour, straining out the micro-organisms in the water as food. Though one oyster might be prettier than the next, the color doesn't affect the quality or flavor. And don't expect to find a pearl. They haven't found one yet.

Although the Tomales Bay Oyster Company supplies two area restaurants, most of their customers are individuals who stop by, much like a farm stand. Several older men come exclusively for the "cowboys," the mammoth, one pound oysters, which they eat on the half shell—raw and whole.

If you want to bring some oysters home, prices range from about $4 per dozen for the small or cocktail oysters to $8 per dozen for the jumbo. So next time you're in the Point Reyes area, stop by the Tomales Bay Oyster Company to test for yourself the health benefits of oysters.

Tomales Bay Oyster Company
Highway 1, 5 miles north of Point Reyes Station
415/663-1242
Open daily 9-5, except Christmas
Free

Extra Tip...To barbecue an oyster, place it flat side up on the grill. On a hot fire, the oyster's shell will crack open. Cut the adductor muscle (that holds the two shells together) with a paring knife. Pry the top shell off, but be careful—it's hot! Dab on barbecue sauce, butter and garlic or seasoning of choice. Cook the oyster over the fire for two to three minutes. Enjoy!

👁 *Anheuser Busch Beer Brewery*

When you tour this massive plant in Fairfield, you'll know why Budweiser is the "King of Beers." This is the largest brewery in the world. You're invited to walk above, around and through the fermenting and bottling buildings. At the end of the tour, you can taste free samples of Anheuser Busch's diverse line of beers, with sodas for the kids.

This brewery produces about 3.7 million barrels of beer every year. Their three bottle lines each fill about 1,000 bottles per minute. The keg line spurts out 600 kegs an hour and 14,000 half-kegs every day. More than that, 1,580 cans are topped off every minute in each of the two can lines. The brewery is abuzz with activity and whirring machinery 24 hours a day, seven days a week, 365 days a year.

The company has come a long way since Eberhard Anheuser acquired a small, debt-ridden brewery in St. Louis, Missouri. His son-in-law, Adolphus Busch, turned it into an industry giant.

Busch introduced Budweiser in 1876 as a new brand created with traditional, time-consuming methods and the finest barley malt, hops and rice. Following that success, he added the Michelob brand in 1896 as "a draught beer for the connoisseurs."

The famous Budweiser Clydesdales first pulled the bright red and green beer wagon in April, 1933 to mark the end of Prohibition. The Clydesdales travelled from the St. Louis brewery to New York's Empire State Building and on to the White House to deliver one of the first post-Prohibition cases of Budweiser. You won't see the Clydesdales at this brewery. Although frequently seen in parades and at fairs, they're kept in other parts of the country.

Today, Budweiser is the largest selling beer in the world, the guide will tell you. A video illustrates the 13-step process involved in creating this King of Beers, from grinding the barley malt and rice to beechwood aging to cold filtering.

The beechwood aging takes place in immense, stainless steel aging tanks stacked three levels high. Just how much beer is in one of these tanks? If you were to drink one case of beer every day for 60 years, you'd just about finish it. A strong odor welcomes you as soon as you step into the aging room. It smells, well, like a brewery.

Before filling the tanks, a worker walks through placing a layer of beechwood chips, which come exclusively from Tennessee, and yeast on the bottom. The beer is added and allowed to age in the tank for 23 to 27 days, depending on the brand. Then it is filtered twice and sent on to bottling.

Most of the process you'll see on the tour is bottle filling and the packaging of beer. Machinery takes up almost all of this cavernous room. Armies of bottles are mechanically removed from boxes and clink and teeter along conveyor belts.

Huge, rapidly spinning silver domes fill the bottles. They are crowned with the metal caps, then march along a conveyor belt to the pasteurizer. Here, they are heated gradually to 120-140° for 45 minutes. Next, they continue to labeling and packaging.

The tour also includes close-ups of the can and keg lines, even the machine that makes case boxes out of flat, printed pieces of cardboard.

Wear comfortable shoes and bring a sweater for the cool, aging room. Also, the machinery is LOUD. But don't worry if you're the designated driver. Anheuser Busch also makes a non-alcoholic beer you can taste at the end of your tour.

Anheuser Busch Brewery Tour
3101 Busch Drive, Fairfield
707/429-2000
Tours Mon.-Fri. 10 & 2
ADVANCE RESERVATION ONLY
Free

Jelly Belly Factory

This is the sweetest deal anywhere. The fascinating behind-the-scenes tour of the Jelly Belly factory, in itself, is worth the trip. But you also get free samples of the candy being produced that day at various stops on the tour. Kids walk away with a free gift, including a gummy item and a poster to color. And you can buy goodies to bring home from the company store, including "belly flops," odd-shaped but just as delicious Jelly Bellies that are sold at about two-thirds less than retail price.

Jelly Bellies are not an ordinary jelly bean. Standard beans only have flavoring in the shell. Jelly Bellies are flavored in the center and in the shell. The secret to their intense, true-to-life taste is the use of all-natural flavors whenever possible. Fruit purees are used in Raspberry, Blueberry and Peach, real peanut butter in Peanut Butter and jalapeno peppers in Jalapeno Jelly Belly beans.

Jelly Belly beans come in 40 gourmet flavors, including Chocolate Fudge, Mai Tai, Buttered Popcorn and Toasted Marshmallow. The most popular are Very Cherry, Green Apple, Coconut, Licorice and Cinnamon.

The Herman Goelitz company, who makes the Jelly Belly, even created a new flavor for their most famous fan, former president Ronald Reagan— Blueberry, in honor of the red, white and blue. Their business boomed during the Reagan years, when a jar of Jelly Bellies was de rigueur in the White House. Three tons of Jelly Bellies were shipped just for the inauguration. This is one highlight of the company's long history.

The Goelitz family first began making candy commercially in 1868. Their most popular product was candy corn, now a Halloween standard. Today, the fifth generation of Goelitz's run the company.

Jelly Bellies, introduced in 1976, are one of their most successful confections. Today, this factory can create more than two million beans per hour and about 100,000 pounds a day at full capacity.

The tour begins with a 15-minute video that illustrates the process and shows close-ups of the machines. The four main ingredients are corn syrup, corn starch, water and sugar. These are made into a liquid "slurry" in the kitchen.

Although the kitchen is not on the tour, you will see where the beans are molded, flavored and coated. As soon as you step through the door, you meet the sweet scents, intricate actions and noises of this magical candy factory.

The first stop is the molding process, where the candies are shaped in trays, 1,260 beans at a time. The tour guide gives everyone a sample of this first stage of Jelly Belly, which is just the center with a light sugar coating.

Nearby, melted chocolate from large pots is sprayed onto nuts and confections as they spin in large barrels. Beyond, rows of stainless steel barrels spin thousands of Jelly Bellies as the colorful, flavored coating is sprayed on. Some candies require a harder coating than others. It takes three weeks to apply all the layers of shell on their special jawbreakers.

Here, the free Jelly Belly samples have all the flavor of the finished product. As you walk through the factory enjoying your Jelly Bellies, you also see where they are quality-checked and "belly flops" are removed. The final stage is the packaging machine.

It takes seven to ten days to create a Jelly Belly, but if you're buying a bag, remember that it probably won't take that long to finish it!

Jelly Belly Factory
Herman Goelitz Candy Company, Inc.
2400 North Watney Way, Fairfield
707/428-2800
Tours Mon.-Fri. 9, 10:15, 11:30; Tu.-Th. 1:30
Reserve in advance; Tours fill a month ahead
Free

👁 *Blue Diamond Almond Factory*

"A can a week" is all they ask and if you don't think you're using your share, consider this: Blue Diamond almond products are found in cereals, candy bars, cookies, ice cream, cosmetics and soap. They are served on planes, Amtrak and the space shuttle. They're shipped to more than 90 countries around the world. The shells alone produce enough energy in their cogeneration plant to run the entire factory plus provide power to 15,000 homes.

The Blue Diamond factory in Sacramento is the largest almond processing plant in the world. In its entirety, the plant covers 90 acres, the equivalent of about 33 city blocks. Fun, informative tours highlight the facility's processing, packaging and shipping departments.

California is the only state that grows almonds commercially. Blue Diamond's origins are rooted back in 1910 when 230 growers formed an exchange. Today, this non-profit cooperative boasts 5,000 almond growers who will harvest about 500 million pounds of nuts each season.

Beginning the last week in August, as many as 7 million pounds of almonds will be brought to the plant for processing every day during harvest.

The tour begins with a 25-minute film, "The Amazing Almond," which recaps the nut's life-cycle, from the crucial bee pollination to the snack bowl. During harvest, growers use large machines to violently shake the trees, causing a hail of nuts to rain down around them.

Each visitor on the tour gets a keepsake paper cap to wear for health regulations. As you enter the processing plant, the aroma of warm almonds draws the group to the blanching machines. Here, the nuts are immersed in 200-degree water so skins can be easily removed. Blanched nuts then are sent over rollers to cool down, dried and placed in cold storage. Nothing is wasted. The skins are recycled as cattle feed.

In another section, rows of quality control workers watch hundreds of nuts roll by and meticulously remove broken or defective pieces. These, too, are not wasted, but used in products that do not require whole nuts. The profits are returned to the growers. Much of the work you'll see on the tour is devoted to this kind of rigorous quality control.

In the packaging department, machines seem in constant motion. Some shoot out small foil packets of almonds for airlines or frozen green beans. Others place labels on cans. Others shrinkwrap boxes. All together, the almond has been in the plant about eight hours from when its shell is first cracked to this last stage.

Blue Diamond grows more than 200 varieties of almonds. The popular Nonpareil accounts for more than half the California crop. It's sold slivered, sliced, blanched, chopped or whole natural. The shorter, plumper Mission variety is used in chocolate bars, ice cream and as snack almonds. The California variety is best for blanching and ideal for cereals and granola bars. Blue Diamond now processes macadamias, hazelnuts and pastachios as well.

In the gift shop, you can taste several flavors of almonds, like spicy smokehouse, barbecue and chili. A favorite with the kids is the candy-coated sample. Bags of nuts, gift boxes and cookbooks are available so you can take a piece of the world's largest almond processing plant home with you.

Blue Diamond Almond Factory
1701 C St., Sacramento
916/446-8409
Tours Mon.-Fri. 10 A.M. and 1 P.M.
Free

Notes

For Kids
of All Ages

Academy of Sciences

The California Academy of Sciences in Golden Gate Park is rated one of the top five natural history museums in the country. You can travel to outer space via the Earth and Space Hall and to the ocean depths through the Steinhart Aquarium. You can even travel back in time through their award-winning exhibit on evolution, then marvel at the diversity of life on Earth today through their natural history dioramas.

An eerie blue aura sets the tone for the Earth and Space Hall. Overhead, our solar system's planets spin as they orbit the sun. Below, a Foucault Pendulum appears to rotate as it swings methodically back and forth. In fact, the pendulum moves along a straight line while the Earth rotates beneath it.

One hands-on exhibit guarantees instant weight loss just by finding out your weight on other planets. Simply step on the scale and push the button. On the moon you'll slim down to low double digits, but on Jupiter you'll be more that twice your weight on Earth. Climb the stairs to the shake table of the Safe Quake exhibit to experience two major earthquakes. Scenes from the disaster movie, "Earthquake," flash on the screen as the floor jolts beneath you.

A walk through the Steinhart Aquarium is the next best thing to SCUBA diving. Dolphins somersault and nod playfully at the children who peer into the tank. Smaller tanks contain everything from the Four-eyed Fish, that can see simultaneously above and below the water as it skims the surface, to the Blind Cave Tetra that has no eyes at all.

The crown jewel of the Aquarium is the 100,000-gallon Fish Roundabout. This circular tank swirls around you as you climb the spiral ramp. Sharks, rays and massive deep ocean fish cruise by inches from where you stand.

To see how this diversity of life evolved, don't miss "Life Through Time." It was named the finest exhibit on evolution in the world by the National Science Foundation. A fossil wall, stretching from floor to ceiling, is the threshold to this voyage back in time. Layers of sediment are dotted with fossils, from the stromatolites of 900 million years ago to a 208-million-year-old theropod dinosaur.

What do a horse and a rhinoceros have in common? Learn about evolutionary ancestors on the interactive computer screens. This state-of-the-art system uses color photos, quizzes and "Life Map" graphs to make learning fun.

As you walk through the millenniums, exhibits show how the first marine vertebrates evolved, why gills became lungs and fins became limbs. Displays include living examples of these evolutionary stages including a lungfish and the amphibious Chinese giant salamander.

A slice of 300-million-year-old forest is inhabited with 8-foot-long millipedes and immense scorpions and dragonflies. The dinosaur age is illustrated with bones and holograms. Weird creatures populate the first stages of the age of mammals.

To find out more about today's mammals, visit the Academy's Wild California room, with its life-like dioramas. Six-foot-tall bull elephant seals roar in a mock "king of the mountain" battle, a deer eyes you warily as you pass her meadow and ducks weave through the marsh. It's just the beginning of what the Academy of Sciences, and the world around us, has to offer.

Academy of Sciences
Golden Gate Park, San Francisco
415/750-7145 (recording)
Open daily 10-5, until 7 P.M. July-Labor Day
$6 Adults; $3 seniors and ages 12-17; $1 ages 6-11
$1 ages 6-11; Free first Wed. of each month

Extra Tip...Save $1 off youth admission. See Bonus Coupon Section.

Cable Car Barn Museum

A trip to San Francisco wouldn't be complete without clinging onto a cable car as it clangs up the steep city streets. But how does it work? And what is that man doing with the huge set of pliers in the middle of the car?

Both kids and adults will have fun learning the answers at the Cable Car Barn Museum at the corner of Mason and Washington streets. Just ask the conductor to call out the stop.

This circa-1907 brick building holds the brawny heart of the world's first mechanized mass transit system, and the last surviving system of its type—the beloved cable car. It's our nation's only moving National Historic Landmark.

As you enter the Museum, head downstairs to the underground viewing room to see the cable enter the powerhouse from beneath the street. Then, follow the constant, vibrating hum upstairs to the balcony overlooking its source. Below, you will see a massive machine. Eight wheels, each 14 feet in diameter, guide and pull the cables for the entire system at a constant 9 1/2 miles per hour.

The cable cars, themselves, have no locomotion. They are pulled by the cables that run beneath the streets of San Francisco. That man on the cable car operating what looked like a huge set of pliers was actually gripping onto the cable to propel the car and letting go of the cable to stop the car. The gripman's job is best demonstrated in the color graphics of the 16-minute video shown continually at the Museum.

It all began in the 1870s with tenacious inventor Andrew S. Hallidie, whose company manufactured wire ropes for the cable railway systems he invented to transport ore in mines.

After witnessing a runaway wagon drag a team of four unfortunate horses down one of the city's steep hills, Hallidie hit upon a new use for his wire rope.

His cable railway system could pull ore up the steep mining grades. Why couldn't an enlarged version transport people over the hills of San Francisco? But like Noah's ark or Tucker's automobile, Hallidie's vision ran into a wall of skeptics who dubbed it "Hallidie's Folly."

Undaunted, Hallidie persuaded a few friends to invest in his dream, threw in all the money he had and sold stock to finance a working model of a cable car.

The official first passenger run of the cable car took place on August 2, 1873. Designed to hold 12 passengers on the grip car and 14 on the coach, 90 glory-seekers squeezed onto the car, starting the tradition of hanging on to the poles. The cable pulled the loaded car successfully up the steep grade. The era of the cable car was launched.

By the late 1800s, San Francisco boasted about 500 cable cars on seven cable car lines requiring 103 miles of track and plenty of Hallidie's wire rope. Cities as far flung as New York, Denver, London and Sydney adopted Hallidie's invention.

At the museum, you can see the first cable car ever built, the same one Andrew Hallidie jockeyed down Clay Street in 1873. The collection of antique cable cars and models illustrates design changes through the years. The cable car you rode on today is the same car our city's forefathers rode at the turn of the century.

After visiting the Museum, take a quick peek into the Cable Car Barn, about 25 feet up Washington Street. It garages the more than 40 cable cars in San Francisco's fleet.

The Cable Car Barn Museum is on both the Powell-Hyde and the Powell-Mason lines. Allow about 1/2 hour for your visit. Cable cars operate from 7:00 A.M. to 12:45 A.M. Rides cost $2 adults (for 2 hours); $1 children 5-17; $.15 for seniors over 65. All-day ride passes cost $6. Tickets can be purchased from the machines at the terminus of each line.

Cable Car Barn Museum
1201 Mason Street, San Francisco
415/474-1887
Open daily 10-5 Nov.-March; 10-6 April-Oct.
Free

Hyde Street Pier

What's the most intriguing site at the San Francisco waterfront? A) Ghiradelli Square B) Pier 39 C) The Cannery D) Hyde Street Pier.

The answer is Hyde Street Pier, a time capsule waiting to be discovered by anyone who veers off the well-travelled tourist beat. Located across the street from the Cannery, thousands of people walk by its unassuming entrance everyday. They don't know what they're missing.

A small fleet of historic ships is berthed here, from the massive, three-masted 1886 Balclutha to the 1890 paddle-wheel ferry Eureka. You're welcome aboard to explore the ships, from the pilot house to the elegant captain's quarters to the cool, dark hold.

Each ship is restored to reflect its heyday. Once aboard the ferry Eureka, you are easily transported to the 1930s when this side-wheeler plied the waters of the Bay. At the time, it was the world's largest passenger ferry, carrying as many as 2,300 people and 120 autos at a time.

Vintage automobiles rest on the wooden planks of the ferry's platform, as though their drivers will return at any moment. Among others, there is a bright red 1937 Diamond T pickup, a blue 1924 Express Wagon, 1933 Packard sedan, a 1931 Model A Ford U.S. mail truck, even a horse-powered wooden wagon marked "D. Ghiradelli Co. Chocolate Cocoa Mustard" and stocked with milk cans.

Through doorways and windows, you can see the ferry's four-story steam engine and its barnacle-encrusted paddlewheels. Upstairs, you can roam through the rows of passenger seats and peer over the counter at the vintage goodies they used to sell during the Bay crossings.

Across the pier, the three-masted, 1895 C.A. Thayer sailed as a lumber cargo ship from the Pacific northwest to California, then, from 1925, as an Alaskan cod fisherman in the Bering Sea. The ship is one of two surviving schooners from a fleet of 900 that once transported lumber to California's rapidly growing cities. Its final trip in 1950 was the last commercial voyage by a west coast sailing vessel.

The 256-foot-long, three-masted Balclutha is an iron and steel sailing ship built in 1886 in Glasgow, Scotland. It sailed around the treacherous Cape Horn five times bringing coal from England and returning with grain. From 1903 to 1930, it made yearly voyages between San Francisco and Alaska to bring salmon south and men and supplies for the canneries north. In the hold, crates of fish are stacked from floor to ceiling.

A museum is in midships, with such artifacts as a helmetdiver's outfit, a collection of anchors and a world map showing the Balclutha's travels to exotic ports like Rangoon, Calcutta and Sydney.

One display describes the unfurling of the top-most sail. This duty usually was handed to a young sailor, who had to climb 130 feet up the mast while the ship pitched and yawed. "Keep your eye on your job," older sailors advised, "and don't look down."

Find out more about the sea at the pier's Maritime Store. It offers one of the city's best selections of books, prints, postcards and more on maritime subjects. You can take a bit of the salt air home with you in one of their audiotapes with music of the sea.

Historic Ships
Hyde Street Pier, San Francisco
415/556-3002
Open daily 10-5
$3 Adults aged 17-61; all others free

Extra Tip...Save $1 off admission to Hyde Street Pier and $1 off admission to the USS Pampanito. See Bonus Coupon Section.

Musée Mécanique & Cliff House

If you want the Nintendo generation to see what mechanical games were like when their grandparents and great grandparents were kids, take them to the Musée Mécanique. This compact fun house is jam-packed with what is probably the world's largest private collection of antique amusements.

All of these 130 or so machines are museum-quality, but instead of ensconcing them behind glass walls, the Musée Mécanique has a hands-on approach. You put coins in the machines to make figures move, find out your fortune or play an early version of pinball, just as your ancestors did more than half a century ago.

Edward Zelinsky and his son, Daniel, are the enthusiastic rescuers and restorers of these mechanical marvels. Some of the games and musical instruments are from Playland-at-the-Beach, which was located nearby. Others came from Europe. The Zelinsky's are constantly adding to the collection.

One of the oldest amusements is the mutoscope from the turn of the century. This was the precursor to motion pictures. Pictures are printed on cards. When the cards are rapidly flipped, the pictures appear to be in motion.

Two of the most intricate and fun machines are the Mechanical Village and Mechanical Farm. A coin brings these miniature worlds to life. Other devices predict your fortune, measure your sexual prowess or play a tune with piano, snare drums, flutes or xylophones.

Two gruesome, miniature working models, dating to late 1930s England, always draw a crowd. One recreates an execution by guillotine, the other by hanging.

Most of the machines leap into motion at the drop of a quarter, but some cost as little as one cent, bringing back the days of the penny arcade.

The museum is located downstairs from San Francisco's Cliff House, which is a prime tourist spot in its own right. Today, hundreds of people stop for the majestic scenery, to explore the ruins of the Victorian-era Sutro baths and to listen to the perpetual barking of the sea lions.

This area perched above the rugged Pacific coastline has been attracting visitors for more than 130 years. It's one of the few places in San Francisco that enjoys that weatherworn, ocean beach air. Where automobiles now vie for parking spaces, carriages once lined up to enjoy the scenery. A character named Captain Foster ran a restaurant here and was well-known for his hospitality and fine food.

Cliff House's popularity weathered financial ebbs and tides in the 1870s. When on the decline in 1883, Adolph Sutro, a Nevada silver king, bought the property. He was determined to make it a top landmark again for the benefit of San Francisco. A journey to the "Cliff" became de rigueur for the Victorian elite.

One of Sutro's most magnificent improvements was the grand, glass-enclosed bathing houses. Swimmers delighted in six sea water and fresh water pools, heated to varying degrees. Bleachers provided seating for thousands of onlookers. Art galleries exercised and cleansed the mind as well.

But the financial tide turned again. The Sutro Baths began losing money and finally closed. A fire burned the abandoned structure in 1966. Today, the ruins below Cliff House are silent reminders of the thousands who once frolicked there.

Musée Mécanique
1090 Point Lobos Ave. (Cliff House), San Francisco
415/386-1170
Open daily 11- dusk
Free; Bring change for the machines

Barbie Doll Hall of Fame

She was an astronaut long before women dreamed it possible. She rides horses, hosts barbecues, drives a sports car, acts on the stage and screen, boasts more shoes than Imelda Marcos and never in her 32 years has grown out of her stunning, cutting edge wardrobe. She is every American's dream girl—Barbie.

At the Barbie Hall of Fame Doll Studio in Palo Alto, you can do more than relive girlhood memories of dressing Barbie in frilly evening gowns and mod bathing suits. Adults discover how the fleeting fads of fashion reflect the current culture. Children marvel at the largest collection of Barbie dolls and accessories in the world.

Owner and operator Evelyn Burkhalter has amassed more than 16,000 items of Barbie memorabilia, "just about everything they've made," she said. She began collecting Barbies in the early 1970s. By 1984, she was able to open her Barbie museum in honor of the doll's 25th anniversary. By 1986, the size of the exhibition doubled. She continues to collect every new Barbie item she can find, which is no easy task. Mattel Toys, Inc. releases at least 50 different Barbies every year.

Display cases are brimming with Barbies dressed in everything from nun's habits to mini-skirts. A short tour around this compact museum will take you from the conservative 1950s to the gold-sequined '90s. There are Ken dolls, diminutive, wide-eyed dolls made for the Japanese market, and white, black, Hispanic, Asian and Native American Barbies. Some commemorate historic events, such as the Friendship Barbie released when the Berlin Wall came down.

Barbie's curvaceous figure first appeared in American toy stores in 1959. Only 1/2 million dolls and 1 million costumes were made. All the original dolls' faces were hand-painted by three artists. They lasted just two months on the market before they were sold out.

Before long, one of Barbie's most popular outfits was the "Suburban Shopper," a starched cotton jumper, wide-brimmed hat, straw tote overflowing with fresh fruits and Barbie's first telephone. In the early 1960s, the Friday Nite Date called for a corduroy jumper with a patchwork scene of a birdhouse in a tree and flowers.

In the late 1960s, Barbie went mod, with a new hairstyle and psychedelic clothes, like the 1969 "Flower Wower" mini-dress in a colorful, giant flower print.

In the 1980s, "they even came out with a Yuppie Barbie," said Burkhalter. Barbie's 1986 Day to Night outfit looked like a business suit by day, but at night the jacket comes off to reveal a shiny dancing dress.

Gift sets also show the history of our culture, ranging from backyard barbecue scenes to a workout gym. Special fashions reflect actual uniforms of the day. Through the years, Barbie has been a flight attendant on a number of airlines. Today, she is the pilot.

Burkhalter has greeted people from around the world to her Barbie Hall of Fame Doll Studio. Her museum has been featured on television and in magazines in Japan, Italy, Amsterdam, France and Sweden, proof that Barbie, the "All-American Girl," is truly a world celebrity.

Barbie Hall of Fame Doll Studio
460 Waverly St., Palo Alto
415/326-5841
Tu.-Fri. 1:30-4:30; Sat. 10:30-Noon & 1:30-4:30
$2 Adults; $1 Children under 12

The Garage

Many Silicon Valley high-tech industries were launched in someone's garage, so it's only fitting that we return to The Garage for an insider's view of what makes computers tick. Even the compu-timid won't be overwhelmed by the museum's fun, hands-on approach to this complex machine.

You can design a bike on a computer, then use a computerized marketing program to calculate how many to stock. Take an air shower and step into the simulated "clean room," where silicon chips are produced. Command a robot arm to spell your name in building blocks. The room is crammed with activity and the weird noises of working machines.

Your first encounter is one of the third kind. A huge model of the Hubble Telescope explains exactly what went wrong. An interactive video screen allows you to direct a flight across the surface of Mars, dipping into valleys and coursing over hills.

Mars may seem far away, but just How Big is Our Universe? A display explains that if our solar system were the size of a postage stamp, then our Milky Way galaxy would be the size of California and the universe would be the size of our solar system.

Back on earth, see how silicon is transformed to mechanical intelligence. You'll have to take an air shower. It's like walking through an airport security metal detector with puffs or air blowing at you from all sides. This is to expel any dust particles. Chips the size of your fingernail may have one million transistors and even one microscopic particle can ruin the chip.

Just took a shower this morning, you say? Step into the phone-booth-sized particle detector and a meter will reveal how many particles your body is emitting. Scratch your head or jump up and down and watch the meter soar.

A six-foot long, enlarged model of a chip shows how it works. Type in your birthdate and it will calculate the day of the week as you follow the steps on the computer screen. The process is slowed to 87 seconds. Normally, it would take 0.012 seconds.

Robotic arms can be a boon to the handicapped. One on display is programmed to answer the phone, get a drink, place food in the microwave and feed a quadriplegic.

An intriguing look into genetic research reveals how these microscopic particles make us who we are. Deformities in genes may be responsible for mental retardation, cataracts and other health problems.

One of the most popular exhibits, especially with high school students, is the bike factory. A three-dimensional imaging system allows you to choose a frame, wheel-type, handlebars and color, then print out your creation to take home with you. You also can try out life-size, high-speed, pedal-powered vehicles. The 1986 "Gold Rush," ridden by Fast Freddy Markham, went over 65 mph for 660 feet.

One exhibit is a provoking collection of industry "artifacts." In 1971, the Victor, a bulky calculator larger than a typewriter, was considered top of the line. It could add, subtract, multiply, divide and remember and sold for $1,995. By 1972, a pocket-size calculator with many more functions sold for $395. Today, a solar-powered, credit-card-size calculator sells for $7. What next? Find out at The Garage.

The Garage
145 West San Carlos, San Jose
(across from Convention Center)
408/279-7150 (recording)
Tues.-Sun. 10-5
$6 Adults; $4 Seniors and ages 6-18

Mystery Spot

Calling all skeptics! Can a golf ball roll uphill? Does a person shrink when nearing the center of the Mystery Spot? Is it all an optical illusion?

Even its name is hokey, but the Mystery Spot is not only fun but intriguing enough to attract the attention of scientists from NASA and Stanford. It is listed in Ripley's Believe It of Not and was photographed for LIFE Magazine. The day I entered the Mystery Spot, visitors from Japan and Hungary as well as the States were thoroughly enjoying this quirky phenomenon.

Deep in the forested hills above Santa Cruz, the Mystery Spot is a 150-foot circle in which gravity seems to be defied. Trees, people and buildings all lean towards the southwest, as though some force was trying to push them downhill. Why?

The scientists have come with their instruments for 50 years, but not one has a definitive answer. Some believed that "The Force" was actually carbon dioxide escaping from a fissure, which would explain why many visitors feel dizzy or seasick.

The most popular explanation is that a very dense meteor crashed here many centuries ago and now lays underground emitting the force that refracts gravity.

It all started when the land was bought for a summer home site. The surveyors' compasses went wild and the workers felt dizzy and top-heavy. Eventually the owner gave up trying to build his home here and opened this strange place to the public.

The enthusiastic guide begins your tour at the outer limits of the Mystery Spot. Two cement blocks are placed about three feet apart. One person stands on the first block, another on the second. When they exchange places, one person shrinks while the other grows taller. Why? One of the cement blocks is inside the Mystery Spot.

A steep climb up a slippery hill—wear non-slip shoes—brings you closer to the center of the Mystery Spot. A ramshackle wooden cabin here is slanted so severely that, if not for the trees holding it up, it would tumble down the hill. The guide leans a board across the windowsill and places a golf ball on it, but instead of rolling down the board, it rolls up it.

An optical illusion you say? The house is crooked so the board looks like it's slanting up when it's really slanting down? The guide pulls out his level. Sure enough, the ball is rolling uphill, or "the force" is pushing it uphill. The guide invites you to try it out with your own level. Unfortunately, I had left mine at home.

Inside the cabin, the guide offers more demonstrations of the mysterious force. Hanging from a handle in the ceiling of the doorway, he looks like someone is pulling his legs to the side. You can try it, too, to see if you look like someone is pulling your leg. A weight hanging from the ceiling in the next room appears heavier when pushed away from the force and lighter when pushed towards the force.

On either side of the cabin are more spots for shrinking and growing as people exchange places. Maybe it's an excess of carbon dioxide, but even skeptics have trouble explaining this one and I can't deny that this really works. Either the guides are very good magicians or there is indeed an unexplainable force inside the Mystery Spot. In any case, this is a fun, unique attraction, "believe it or not."

The Mystery Spot
1953 Branciforte Dr., north of Santa Cruz
408/423-8897
Open daily 9:30-5 (last tour at 4:30)
$3 Adults; $1.50 ages 5-11

Extra Tip...Save 15% off admission. See Bonus Coupon Section.

Bocce Ball, Biking & Birdwatching

Bocce ball, biking, birdwatching, boating, even BMX-boosting and a whole lot of outdoor fun that doesn't start with a "B" awaits you at the Martinez Regional Shoreline. This 343-acre park has soccer and softball fields, a playground, a duck pond, horse arena, marina, fishing pier, exercise course and quiet trails through a salt marsh.

Bocce is one of the most popular sports at the Shoreline. The Martinez Bocce Federation is one of the largest Bocce organizations west of the Mississippi. More than 1,000 Bocce aficionados play in Martinez on 110 teams. Several national bocce champions hail from Martinez. The Northern California Open Bocce Championship is held on these courts, usually in July.

No longer reserved for old Italian men, Bocce Ball is a fun, social sport for the whole family. Men, women and children play almost every day of the week at this shoreline park.

Here you can practice the sport of Bocce on no less than 12 regulation-size, clay and ground oyster-shell courts. If you don't have your own set of balls, you can rent them for $10 per day from the Martinez Recreation Department (tel. 510/372-3510). It's a good idea to reserve ahead as they only have two sets and be prepared to leave a $55 returnable deposit.

If you're not sure of the rules, these are the highlights. There are traditionally two teams of four players each, eight Bocce balls and one pallino, or target ball. The game starts with one player rolling the pallino, a lemon-sized ball, down the court. Then she rolls a Bocce ball, about the size of a grapefruit, as near to the pallino as possible.

The opposing team member tries to roll his Bocce ball closer to the pallino than his opponent's. He also might knock hers out of the way or knock the pallino away. His team continues to roll until one of their balls is closer or all four of his team's balls are rolled.

The team with the Bocce ball nearest the pallino scores a point for that Bocce ball and for each of their Bocce balls that are closer to the pallino than their opponents' nearest ball. It is possible to score four points in one round. The game is played to 12 points. Three games are played for each match.

Some players in Martinez play by the "International" rules, using brass balls that can be tossed through the air rather than rolled as in the more popular "Open" rules.

If all this sounds confusing, don't worry. There's usually an avid player nearby to explain the scoring and offer tips on how to aim and roll the balls. Picnic tables between the courts offer spectators comfortable seats and a place for refreshments.

Kids also will enjoy playing catch on the Joe DiMaggio ball fields, named after the Martinez native who became famous playing for the New York Yankees. Kite flying and picnicking also are fun activities on the park's lawns.

Down by the shoreline, visit the quacking ducks and honking geese at the duck pond. A walk to the end of the old-fashioned wooden fishing pier offers a view of the massive steel Carquinez bridge. For the quieter side of this family park, follow the paths west along the shoreline through the marsh.

To top off your day, save time to explore Martinez' downtown. The many antique stores are brimming with fun and unusual knick knacks.

Martinez Regional Shoreline
Follow signs from downtown Martinez
510/228-0112 (Park Office-for marsh questions)
510/372-3510 (City Recreation Office-
for bocce, softball, soccer and BMX questions)
Open daily
Free

Lawrence Hall of Science

Have you ever wondered how supermarket scanners work? How primitive Polynesians could navigate across vast stretches of ocean? Or how you can detect the scent of fresh-baked cookies?

With a fun, hands-on approach, the Lawrence Hall of Science shows how science affects everyday lives, even before the word "science" was invented. You can sail an ancient Polynesian craft by computer, create your own laser show, walk inside a huge, electrified model of the human brain and much more. Younger kids will delight in some of the displays and games. Most exhibits are geared to complicated processes that will fascinate the serious student and intrigued adult.

This modern, low-slung building sits on a lofty perch high above the UC Berkeley campus. The view alone is worth the curvy drive up the hill. On a clear day, you can see San Francisco, parts of Marin and almost the entire East Bay.

The Lawrence Hall presents science on a human level. In The Wayfinding Art, models of Polynesian sailing ships illustrate the simplicity in design—a platform stretched between two hollow pontoons.

How do we know where these people sailed? The study of linguistics and archeology determines the common roots of the residents of many south Pacific lands. Press a button to hear how similar the word "fish" or "eye" is in Tagalog and other languages. "Canoe Do It?" challenges you to sail to an island via computer. You're given a limited number of days and provided with daily reports on wind and weather changes.

Another room is devoted to the laser. A cutaway of a supermarket scanner reveals how lasers are used in this fast, new method of totalling the cost of your groceries and keeping inventory at the same time. The laser "reads" the UPC code, that square of black and white vertical lines on the carton, that carries all this information.

Lasers also create holograms, three-dimensional images that defy their flat frames. As you walk by one hologram, a hand stretches out to grab you then waves as you cross by. The most confounding hologram is a pair of binoculars protruding from the wall. Lean forward and peer into the nebulous eyepieces to see a binocular's magnified point of view of a snake and parrot on the branches beyond.

Ophthalmologists use lasers to detect vision problems. With the equipment here you can see a magnified image of your eye on a television monitor or look at microscopic white blood cells dancing across the surface of your eye.

The key to learning these fun aspects of science is centered in your brain, the subject of another fascinating exhibit. A video shows a woman dissecting a human brain, explaining how certain sections of this mass of tissue help you smell, see, hear and learn.

Inside an immense model of the brain, an interactive computer shows how the simple actions of Little Red Riding Hood employ parts of the brain. When she smells cookies baking, a light flashes on the section of the brain model that controls smell.

On weekends, you can peek inside the flight deck and living quarters of a space shuttle model. In the Discovery Labs, you can stand your hair on end with static electricity, compare your heartbeat with a rabbit's and experiment with pendulums and motors.

The Planetarium offers shows on the constellations. On Saturday nights, you can see the stars and planets first-hand when amateur astronomers meet on the museum's patio.

Lawrence Hall of Science
Centennial Dr., UC Berkeley
510/642-5132 (recording)
Mon.-Fri. 10-4:30; Sat. & Sun. 10-5
$4 Adults; $3 Seniors 62 and over and Students 7-18
or college with I.D.; Prices may be less depending
on exhibits and time of year.

Lindsay Museum

The Lindsay Museum in Walnut Creek specializes in small miracles. Here you can meet a bobcat who would have died in the wild. You can see a young boy, at first terrified of snakes, reach out to pet one. You might even notice a raccoon being taken for a walk.

These are some of the more than 9,000 injured, mistreated or abandoned native wild animals that are brought to the Lindsay Museum each year. Whether it's a deer hit by a car, a raptor that struck electrical wires or a chick that fell from its nest, the ultimate goal is to heal the animal, then return it to the wild.

The 100 native wild animals that reside permanently at the Lindsay were saved but would not survive if returned to their natural habitat. Some are irreparably injured. Others have been "imprinted," which occurs at an early age when the animal bonds to a person, rather than its own kind.

Today they greet 100,000 visitors each year and are vital to the Lindsay's goal to teach people to live responsibly and in harmony with nature.

The Lindsay is a natural history museum for all ages, where people and animals work together. Young interpretive guides bring snakes, owls and other animals out of their glass-enclosed homes to give visitors an "up close and personal" approach.

These young teens work wonders with the small children who visit, teaching them fun facts such as snakes are smooth, not slimy, and they smell with their tongues. Sometimes, they show off one of the two resident barn owls, pointing out how their eyes don't rotate, but their heads can turn nearly all the way around. About 65 baby barn owls are brought to the Museum each year, then released as soon as they can make it on their own.

Some animals, like the bobcat, are strictly for viewing. The animals' care, comfort and safety is

#1 at the Lindsay, before any educational programs or display plans. They are loved, but they're treated like wild animals.

The Lindsay's permanent residents include an opossum, a raven, a red fox, squirrels, a black-tailed hare, a raccoon, a painted turtle, a kestrel and more. Not all animals are on display all the time. Each is given routine "rest and recreation" vacations on a ranch in Martinez.

The Lindsay's science exhibits emphasize the "please touch" approach. Discovery boxes, with intriguing labels like "How Old Am I?" and "Imagine the Gall" invite children and adults to learn more about the natural world around them. Stick your hand in the "Feely Boxes" and try to identify a skull or a rock by touch.

Local children can check out "Natural History to Go" specimens, such as a mounted tree frog. Members of the Pet Library have access to 90 domestic rabbits, hamsters, guinea pigs and rats. They can take these animals home for a week of intimate learning, if they follow instructions and pass a written test on the animal's care.

The Lindsay Museum's phone consultation service receives about 20,000 calls each year. They advise people who have found injured opossums or baby birds dropped from the nest. Sometimes, the animal needs to be brought immediately to Lindsay's hospital. Often the caller should leave the animal alone and observe it. For example, fledglings, baby birds that have developed feathers, need several days on the ground before they learn to fly.

Most importantly, the Lindsay Museum invites all of us to take a closer look at the wild animals right in our own back yard.

Lindsay Museum
1901 First Ave. (in Larkey Park), Walnut Creek
510/935-1978
Wed.-Sun. 1-5; Wed.-Sun. 11-5 in summer
Free; Donations appreciated

Oakland Museum

What do the barn owl, Mickey mouse and landscape artist Thomas Hill have in common? They are all part of the unique heritage of the great state of California.

The Oakland Museum is a whirlwind tour of California's environment, history and art. This is one of the best organized museums anywhere. The first floor is devoted to California's natural history, cutting a swath of the state from seashore to mountaintop. The second floor encapsulates man's history, from Native Americans to Hollywood. The third showcases California art through the decades, from landscapes to modernism.

Begin on the first floor with the dizzying film, "Fast Flight." In five minutes, you rocket from the pounding surf, over the coastal mountains, across the central valley, up the crest of the Sierra and down to the deserts.

Now you can take a leisurely walk across California from west to east. Each mini-environment, from seashore to Sierra, captures life-like scenes of animal, plant and insect life to illustrate the interactions of nature.

The diorama of the mountain lion resting by its recently killed deer demonstrates the food chain. Energy from the sun is used by the green plants, which are eaten by the deer, which is eaten by the lion, then returned to the earth as waste.

Other exhibits include a redwood grove alive with bird songs, a weasel attacking a porcupine and a bear eating berries. There is one live display, a squeamish termite farm. Another is proof that "some living things survive mainly by irritating other livings things," that is, galls on trees.

The History Floor boasts the most comprehensive holding of California memorabilia anywhere. On interactive touch screens, computers describe the more than 6,000 artifacts in the gallery.

Along the three-dimensional time-line, you will walk past the Indians' acorn granaries, ceremonial regalia and basketry to the Spanish missionary era's illuminated Bibles and embroidered garments.

The "Goldseekers and Adventurers" section has a complete assayers' office, with counter, workshop, scales and log books. This is the original James J. Ott's Assayers Office from Nevada City. Other objects include dredges, playing cards, photographs, gold nuggets and much more.

The crude lifestyle of the forty-niners contrasts sharply with the intricate, graceful Victorians. One fancy lady greets a dandy on his big-wheeled bicycle at her door. The door is framed with sparkling etched glass.

As you walk through the 20th century, you realize that you, too, share a place in California's history. Peek into a 1940s kitchen, a 1960s patio barbecue with grilling steaks, a cheese tray, wines and peach pie, and a 1980s den with Scandanavian-style black leather furniture and Trivial Pursuit.

The 20th century is the most technically marvelous, and cluttered, of all, with stylized motorcycles, surfboards, Apple computers, movie cameras and windmills. The hippies earned a display, with candles, psychedelic album covers and a guitar patterned with "Peace and Love." Even the Yuppies are represented by a woman's gray business suit, white blouse, red bowed scarf and a laminated I.D. card from Bechtel.

The third floor highlights California art and artists. The collection includes masterful landscapes of Yosemite by Thomas Hill. Early 20th-century work is characterized by the California Decorative Style, including a stunning, stained glass window. More recent works include flowing three-dimensional sculptures and the vibrant colors of contemporary artists.

Oakland Museum
1000 Oak St. (at 10th St.), Oakland
510/834-2413 (recording)
Wed.-Sat. 10-5; Sun. noon-7
Free, contributions appreciated

Tilden Regional Park

Tilden is perfect for families with small children, romantic couples, hardy hikers, nature lovers— anybody who enjoys a day outdoors. This regional park boasts an 18-hole golf course, Little Farm complete with goats, a pig and other animals, a swimming beach, old-fashioned carousel, scenic picnic grounds, botanic garden, miniature steam train and miles of nature and wilderness trails.

Tilden covers 2,078 acres, so you may have to drive to different activities. You might want to start at the south end of the park and take a ride on the miniature steam train. It delights kids of all ages as it chugs through the trees. (Open Sat., Sun. & holidays 11-6 year-round; Mon.-Fri. 12-5 during school spring and summer vacations, weather permitting. $1.25/ride, $5/5 rides, tel 510/548-6100.)

You can follow South Park Drive through Tilden past a series of picnic grounds to the Botanic Garden. It was founded in 1940, making it almost as old as Tilden, itself. This garden is devoted to the collection, growing, display and preservation of California's native plants.

Gardeners have squeezed 160,000 square miles of California into this 10-acre botanic monument. Paths meander through a surprising diversity of shapes, textures and colors in the plant kingdom.

Regional plant communities include Shasta-Cascade, Channel Islands, Pacific Rain Forest, Coastal Dunes and many more. Every month offers something special, whether it be March's California poppies, August's evening-primroses or the first manzanita blooms in mid-December. (Open daily 10-5 except Christmas; tel. 510/841-8732; Free)

On a hot day, enjoy a dip in cool Lake Anza. There are picnic grounds nearby and a small sandy beach for laying in the sun. Lifeguards are on duty from 11 A.M. to 7 P.M. (Open daily May-Oct.; Swim fee $2 Adults; $1 for under 15, 62 and over and disabled persons; under 1 free; tel. 510/848-3385)

Don't miss the old-fashioned merry-go-round near the end of Lake Anza Road. This treasure was built in 1911 and is one of only 20 existing "menagerie-type" Herschell-Spillman carousels. It once delighted visitors to San Bernadino Ocean Beach. You can ride on a fantastical tiger, ostrich, giraffe, lion, a traditional horse, a rocking carriage and many more unique creatures and seats.

The vintage pipe organ plays gay tunes as the carousel twirls around. In front, a carved wooden band leader keeps time by waving her baton. Take a peek in back to see the percussion system at work. Mechanisms cause sticks to hit drums to the beat.

Another favorite with kids is the Little Farm, with all the sights, sounds and smells of the country. It even has a kid-size red barn and wind mill. Cows, sheep, pygmy goats, a pig and more domestic animals welcome visitors to their farm. Ducks have found a home in the pond nearby.

You can even bring vegetables to feed the cows, pigs and other farm animals, but please don't give them fruit, crackers and bread products and don't pick plants growing nearby—some may be poisonous.

This is all part of the 740-acre nature study area, which also encompasses several short (1/2-mile to mile-long) trails ranging from gentle to steep. You're sure to find a walk that's just what you are looking for to get back to nature.

Tilden Regional Park
Berkeley Hills
(follow signs from Grizzly Peak Blvd.)
510/525-2233
Free

Snoopy & Skating

Who is one of the most recognizable Americans in the world today? That ace pilot, bird-loving beagle, Snoopy! He was on the cover of LIFE, went to the moon with Apollo 10 and shook hands with Prince Charles. Every day, more than 100 million people around the world enjoy Snoopy's antics in over 2,000 newspapers translated into 26 languages.

You'd think a beagle of such bearing would be created in New York, Paris or Milan, but he's drawn right here in Santa Rosa by one of the town's most famous residents, Charles Schultz.

Schultz, the creator of Snoopy, Charlie Brown and the rest of the Peanuts gang, has provided the public with a slice of Peanuts paradise in his hometown.

You can relive the history of Peanuts through the awards, original drawings and memorabilia in Snoopy's Gallery. You can buy a Peanuts toy in the gift shop, which features the largest collection of Snoopy merchandise in the world. And you can enjoy Schultz' second love, ice skating, in the rink next door.

Since he was a small child growing up in Minneapolis, Schultz knew that only one career was right for him—that of a cartoonist. He was inspired by his father, who made sure they bought all four Sunday papers published in the area so they could read the comics. Schultz realized his dream when he sold his first Peanuts comic strip to United Feature Syndicate on October 2, 1950.

The original drawing for this first strip, hanging in the gallery, reveals that the initial Peanuts gang was much more simply drawn. The characters have full, round faces and Charlie Brown's jersey has no trademark zig-zag stripe. Through the progression of original drawings, you can see how the kids developed.

Other memorabilia includes a model of Apollo 10, in which Snoopy and Charlie Brown went to the moon as mascots in 1969. Color animation cels, layers of plastic sheets with a series of drawings, show how Peanuts television specials are made. A note from Ronald Reagan contains his sketch of a cowboy. Its postscript reads, "As you can see, I'm no threat to you in your chosen work."

Downstairs, Peanuts and Snoopy toys span every marketing idea imaginable. Barrettes, neckties, alarm clocks, flashlights, fire engines, embroidery kits, plush toys, t-shirts, mugs, music boxes and many more items feature the familiar Peanuts figures.

Next door, Schultz' Redwood Ice Arena looks like a colorful Swiss Chalet. Like the Peanuts gang, Schultz created this rink to provide hours of fun, old-fashioned entertainment for the whole family. It's a good idea to call ahead to confirm the rink's public hours, especially in December when it hosts a show of world-class skating stars. If the kids have more energy than Mom and Dad on the ice, a coffee shop offers a place to relax looking out on the skaters.

Snoopy Gallery and Gift Shop
1667 West Steele Lane, Santa Rosa
707/546-3385
Open daily 10-6
Free

Redwood Empire Ice Arena
next door to Snoopy Gallery
Winter Hours (Sept.-April):
Mon. 12:30-2 & 8:30-10:30 (Adults only);
Tu. 4-5:30; Wed. 12:30-2;
Th. 4-5:30 & 7:30-9; Fri. 4-5:30 & 8-10:30;
Sat. 12:30-2:30, 3-5 & 8-10:30;
Sun. 12:30-2:30 & 3-5;
Longer hours in summer.
707/546-7147
$5 Adults; $4.50 ages 12-17; $4 ages 11 and under
Skate Rental: $1.50

🚂 *California State Railroad Museum*

It claims to be the "finest railroad museum in North America." After visiting, you might question that claim. This is certainly one of the finest railroad museums in the world.

In 100,000 square feet of exhibit space, you can explore above, on board and below 21 beautifully restored locomotives and cars. The collection includes Central Pacific's first locomotive, Lucius Beebe's luxurious private railcar, a post office car where you can try sorting mail, an immense, 1,051,200-pound steam engine and the St. Hyacinthe sleeping car that recreates high-speed night travel through deceivingly realistic special effects.

The California State Railroad Museum is located where railroading in the west all began—in Old Sacramento. With the financing of the Big Four, the labor of 10,000 Chinese, the determination of Manifest Destiny and the inspiration of a nation, California was linked to the rest of the country via the transcontinental railroad on May 10, 1869.

The first room in the museum is dedicated to this astonishing accomplishment. The shiny black, gray and brass 1862 "Gov. Stanford," Central Pacific Locomotive No. 1, appears to chug through a snowy Sierra scene. Chinamen lift barrels of blasting powder up perilously steep cliffs. A whistle blows in the background, heralding a new era in transportation and history.

The main exhibit hall showcases most of the restored locomotives, some more works of art than machine. The passenger cars of the late 1800s are equally elaborate. Peek into Nevada Central Railway's "Silver State" to see ornately painted details, upholstered seats, wooden louvered shutters and a wood stove. Even Virginia and Truckee's typical 1873 freight locomotive, "Empire," boasts brass trim, bright red wheels and gold-emblazoned lettering.

The giant of all steam locomotives is Southern Pacific's No. 4294. Towering three times taller than the average person, this 1944 million-pound, 6,000 horsepower Goliath is the sole survivor of these unique cab-forward engines.

Step aboard Canadian National Railways' "St. Hyacinthe" Pullman to relive train travel of the 1930s. The gentle rocking of the car, crossing lights flashing by the window and sounds of the rails and whistles all add to the illusion. Berths are lowered from the ceiling, hand towels wait by the stainless steel sinks in the washroom and thick, burgundy curtains are pulled closed for privacy.

Lucius Beebe's railcar, "The Gold Coast," marked the epitome in private rail travel. In 1948, this bon vivant hired a Hollywood decorator to refurbish an 1890s business car. With opulent furnishings, chandeliers, a fireplace and fine silver and china, Beebe brought back rail travel in a grand manner.

You can try sorting mail on the Great Northern Railway Post Office Car. It operated as a complete U.S. Post Office on wheels between Chicago and Tacoma, Washington. Armed clerks sorted letters while the train sped as fast as 80 mph. An ingenious arm swings out to catch sacks full of mail hanging on poles by the side of the track.

In addition to this exceptional collection, films, artifacts, souvenirs, informative displays, hands-on quizzes and enthusiastic docents all add to this unique monument to the railroad and its place in American history.

California State Railroad Museum
2nd and I Sts., Old Sacramento
916/448-4466
Open daily 10-5
$5 Adults; $2 ages 6-17
Includes same-day admission to
the Central Pacific Railroad Depot

🚂 *Travis Air Force Museum*

If man were meant to fly, he'd have wings like these. In the parking lot in front of the Travis Air Force Museum are more than 20 aircraft of every size, shape and design. There's a Globemaster II C-124 large enough to carry a tank, a double-rotor rescue helicopter, a huge B-52D bomber and a sleek Phantom II jet.

Inside the museum, you'll find more airplanes, from the Gonzales Aeroplane No. 1, dating to 1910, to World War II-era trainers. There's even a collection of NASA spacecraft models. You can climb into one capsule and flip toggle switches to feel what it was like to be one of our first astronauts.

This surprising collection is located on Travis Air Force Base in Fairfield. As you tour the historic planes, you often see and hear their modern-day counterparts taking off and landing on a nearby strip.

One of the museums' newest additions is a Russian-made Iraqi anti-aircraft gun captured after a major tank battle at Kuwait City International airport. Many more of the exhibits are from World War II and the 1950s and 1960s.

The collection includes a series of bomb casings, including the stubby, 10-foot, 8-inch long "Fat Man" casing for the atomic bomb dropped on Nagasaki on August 9, 1945.

One intriguing artifact is the cockpit of a Waco CG-4 Assault Glider. With canvas stretched over steel, these lightweight gliders were towed by C-47 aircraft to a target area. Once there, they could land silently in an open field. The gliders could carry 15 troops or eight troops and one jeep and 90% made only one assault landing.

The Gonzales Aeroplane No. 1, used in San Francisco in 1910-1912, looks like something the Wright Brothers flew. It is little more than a seat and 35 horsepower engine attached to 36-foot wingspan and a tail, totalling 28 feet long. Designed primarily as a trainer, the plane boasted a top speed of 132 mph and a range of 450 miles.

Compare this to the impenetrable-looking B-52D, one of the huge aircraft parked outside the museum. B-52s, used extensively in the late 1960s and early 1970s, have a wingspan of 185 feet, more than five times wider than the Gonzales. They reach speeds up to 638 mph and weigh more than 220 tons.

Another giant is the Globemaster II C-124, the first of which flew in 1949. This aircraft is almost five stories tall and could transport tanks, bulldozers and trucks or carry 200 soldiers in its double-decker cabin. A door in its nose lowers for easy loading and there's an elevator under its aft fuselage.

An unusual aircraft is the Grumman HU-16 Albatross. This amphibian was designed to operate from land, water and snow, with skis. It is best known for its rescues, often behind enemy lines, in Korea and Southeast Asia.

One of the most contemporary aircraft on display is the McDonnell Douglas F-4C Phantom II. It entered into service in 1961 as a fleet defense interceptor for the U.S. Navy. This jet could reach 1,400 mph and boasted a range of 1,750 miles. When used by the Air Force in Southeast Asia, it could carry twice the bomb load of the World War II-era B-17.

This is just the beginning of what the Travis Air Museum has to offer. You also can see aircraft under restoration, engines, a collection of pilots' helmets through the years or watch movies that show many of these planes in action.

Travis Air Force Museum
Travis Air Force Base, Fairfield
707/424-5605
Mon.-Fri. 9-4; Sat. 9-5; Sun. Noon-5
Free

Western Railway Museum

Clang, clang, clang goes the trolley—straight into nostalgia and fun at the Western Railway Museum. It's like playing with your old train set, but this is life-sized..

People line up at the depot. The trolley pulls away with a clickety-clack and a gleeful ring. It rumbles past an immense locomotive and freight cars stretching into the prairie, then circles back to the stop at the railroad barn with its impressive collection of antique and unusual engines and coaches.

The museum isn't exactly on the beaten path, but it's worth the drive along Highway 12 past rolling hills and sheep herds When you arrive, you'll find several enthusiastic volunteers, complete in conductor uniforms. They are part of the 1,000-member, non-profit Bay Area Electric Railroad Association who share their love of railroads through this museum.

Begin your tour with a ride on one of the four antique electric railway cars, such as the car that originally ran across the San Francisco Bay Bridge. These cars have been completely restored, some to the tune of 10,000 or more volunteer man-hours. Inside you'll find polished wood paneling and vintage advertisements. You can watch and ask questions as the conductor works the crank and bell.

The trolley rumbles past a yard piled with rusted railroad parts, but "whatever you do, don't call that junk," our conductor, Al Lingo, explained. "That's gold." The association avidly collects old railroad cars and parts that have been left to rot in yards and fields.

In the carbarn, you can see how these "junked" railroads can come back to life. Some have pictures that show their original state. Of the thirty cars in the barn, several have been restored. Others may never be revived.

Children especially enjoy climbing onto and through the cars. You can even ring the bell on some, if you do it gently. Old-timers will recognize the design of several of the cars that used to be part of the Bay Area's Key System. The System, and some of the cars here, dates back to the turn of the century, and encompassed San Francisco ferry boats that connected with East Bay electric trains and streetcars.

An unusual specimen is the Blackpool Corporation Transit or Boat Car. This open-air, boat-shaped car was built in England in 1934 for use in Blackpool, a seaside resort. Tourists enjoyed this unique form of transportation along the coast, complete with slatted wooden seats to accommodate wet bathing suits.

Another passenger car had traveled more than 1.2 million miles on the streets of Melbourne, Australia before coming to San Francisco for the 1983 Historic Trolley Festival. A Koala painted on the side of the car invites people to "Hop Aboard, Mate."

A favorite with the kids is the classic caboose, this one from the Great Northern Railroad. Built about 1899, cabooses originally were used as quarters for the train crews. A person riding in the cupola could watch the freight cars for mechanical problems. Today, the crew rides in the diesel locomotive and cabooses are no longer needed.

If the Railway Museum has sparked your enthusiasm for the rails, stop by their bookstore with its extensive collection of railroad publications or picnic at their landscaped grounds by the trolley tracks.

The Western Railway Museum
Highway 12 (10 mi. east of Fairfield)
Solano County
707/374-2978
Sat. & Sun. 11-5
$4 Adults; $2 ages 4-15

Notes

Asian Art Museum

The largest museum outside Asia devoted to Asian art is right here in San Francisco. The Asian Art Museum in Golden Gate Park has an estimated 12,000 works spanning more than 6,000 years. The works are intriguing, from the tiny oracle bones to large earthenware sculptures to the world's oldest dated Buddha known to exist.

Even if you're a not a Buddhist, several works are supplemented with fascinating histories that will enlighten you. Upstairs, thoughtfully organized galleries travel from Cambodia through Vietnam, ancient India, Japan and Tibet. Buddhas, porcelains and bronzes exhibit the distinctive, intricate Asian craftsmanship.

Downstairs, this museum's collection of Chinese and Korean art is world famous. Their extensive selection of jade encompasses many pieces from 10th to 15th-century China.

Among the Chinese artifacts, one rare piece is barely noticeable, a finger-length sliver of bone from a cow's scapula. Markings on the bone reveal that it is an Oracle Bone of Shang. From 1200 to 1050 B.C., diviners expressed a wish or question, applied a hot brand to the bone to crack it, then divined the answers. Oracle Bones were used for decisions in everyday life, from agriculture to travel.

More importantly, oracle bones tell historians that this was the first fully literate civilization east of the Indus Valley and the first users of script which characterizes the writing of Chinese and Far Eastern languages.

A three-foot-tall glazed earthenware camel from the 8th century tells another story. This kind of object was placed in tombs of royalty, such as that of Princess Yongtai.

Born in 684, Yongtai's ruthless grandmother captured the seat of Empress through marriage, intrigue and assassination, eliminating all her rivals to the throne. At 17, Yongtai was her victim, her body thrown in a lime pit to conceal the murder. When the Empress was dethroned, Yongtai's body was recovered and placed in an immense tomb along with more than 1,000 objects, all of which remain in China as national treasures.

Second-floor galleries focus on other Asian cultures. Almost all the works are inspired by religion. Many are Buddhas or Bodhisattvas, those who have renounced the rewards of enlightenment to remain on Earth and help mankind.

An unusual collection from Tibet features 18th-century human bone implements, such as thigh-bone trumpets and skull bowls. To the Buddhist, the display explains, human bones are reminders that life is brief and death inevitable. Tibetans saw the skull as a "natural container" unshaped by human hands. It represents the fundamental goodness that is the natural condition of the mind.

Artworks from Japan are refined, elegant and graceful. A large, mid-19th-century kago, used to carry a person, is black and red lacquer with gold highlights. Painted screens show the beauty in simplicity, a concept that prevails in many of the works exhibited in this exceptional museum.

Asian Art Museum
Golden Gate Park, San Francisco
415/668-8921
Open Wed.-Sun. 10-5;
Open 10 A.M.-8:45 P.M.first Wed. of each month
$5 Adults; $3 Seniors 65 and over; $2 ages 12-17
Includes same-day admission to de Young
Free first Sat. morning 10-Noon
and first Wed. of each month.

Chinese Historical Society

Did the Chinese land in America before Columbus? The Spanish recorded a Chinese presence in California as early as the 1630s. After the gold rush, the Chinese made up 90% of the Central Pacific's workforce during the construction of the transcontinental railroad. In 1882, 75% of California's agricultural workers were Chinese.

You can learn this and more about the Chinese role in California's history at the Chinese Historical Society in San Francisco. Don't be put off by its unassuming entrance and off-the-beaten-path location. Although compact, the museum offers unique insight into the Chinese experience through displays, historical photographs and such artifacts as a full-size fishing boat, a century-old altar and a traditional braid of hair, called a queue.

Displays look into the good and bad sides of Chinese history. A long opium pipe is symbolic of the many troubles that nation suffered because of this drug. Widespread addiction led to the First Opium War, a defeat to England and a century of foreign domination.

Gold! It lured white settlers from across the country and thousands of Chinese from across the Pacific. In 1850, only 450 Chinese lived in San Francisco. Two years later, the number exploded to 20,000. After 1852, an average of 10,000 Chinese immigrated every year.

Most came from Canton, the only open port in China. Because of the country's closed door policy, the rest of China didn't know about the gold rush, or couldn't get out if they did.

Those that did come held on to their heritage, culture and language. The queue, a long braid of hair, was worn by men as a symbol of their allegiance to the Manchu Emperor of China. After a revolution in 1911, they cut their queues. Another display shows the tools and plants used by a traditional herb shop for medicinal uses.

The most colorful artifact is the immense dragon head. Made in Canton, it was shipped here in 1911 for use in parades and was one of the first dragon heads to be equipped with electric lights. The century-old, deep red altar was carved by Chinese laborers for their temple in Napa.

Through hard work, the Chinese were able to create new and successful industries only to be forced out by discriminatory practices and laws. One such industry was shrimp farming, as represented by the museum's massive wooden winnowing machine.

Some Chinese brought the skills they learned in America back home with them. Displays tell the stories of people like Chin Gee Hee, who worked on the railroad here. He returned to his home town in 1905 to build a railroad for his countrymen. It served the community for 20 years until the Japanese destroyed it in World War II.

From the museum, it's a short walk to the heart of Chinatown. Portsmouth Square, now landlocked by the financial district, was once the harbor where Chinese first landed in San Francisco during the gold rush. Today, groups of Chinese men cluster around boisterous games of tiles and cards.

On the busy streets of this community, you'll find colorful vegetable stands filled with such unusual produce as lotus root or mile-long beans. In a tea shop, you can try a cup of ginseng tea, believed to have many health benefits. Shops are brimming with fun, inexpensive Chinese imports and reasonably priced gifts, embroidered linens and silk clothing. To top it off, sample the exotic foods of the orient for a true taste of San Francisco's Chinese heritage.

Chinese Historical Society
650 Commercial St., near Kearny, San Francisco
415/391-1188
Tu.-Sat. Noon-4
Free, contributions appreciated

Coit Tower

Coit Tower was never intended to resemble a firehose nozzle, but there is no better way to describe this cylindrical, fluted tower that tops Telegraph Hill. There is, however, much more to this structure than its art deco shape and panoramic view from the top.

Lining both sides of Coit Tower's circular lobby are provocative murals that immortalize one of our nation's most difficult eras. It was the 1930s, a time of harsh, industrial working conditions for those who had jobs and little hope for those who didn't. The murals portray the working class, from the factories to farms.

The murals were painted about sixty years ago. A massive and meticulous restoration process has pumped new life into the artworks' vibrant colors. For $1, the Coit Tower brochure describes each of the murals and the history of the tower. Although its map is a bit confusing, the text offers a deeper appreciation for the murals' message.

Coit Tower was originally built as a monument to Lillie Hitchcock Coit, one of San Francisco's most colorful women. In the late 1800s, Lillie often dressed as a man to gamble in North Beach saloons. She smoked cigars and publicly ice-skated in shortened skirts.

Lillie was best known for her passion for firefighting. In 1863, Knickerbocker Hose Company #5 declared Lillie their mascot and she rarely missed a blaze. Coit Tower is a result of her $125,000 bequest to San Francisco.

The murals were commissioned by the U.S. Government as a Public Works of Art Project, but they later regretted it. The social criticism prevalent in these artworks caused a controversy that delayed the opening of the tower from May until October 1934.

Although 25 artists worked on the murals, they are surprisingly homogeneous in style and theme.

These actually are frescoes. They are the result of a time-consuming, tricky process in which dry pigments are applied with a wet brush to fresh plaster.

The social realists combined scenes of everyday life with sobering touches of unadorned reality. The colors are bold, the portraits stark, the expressions somber. Each tells a story of the working class.

One depicts the stages of a newspaper, from reporters gathering news, to typesetters, to the newsboy selling the finished product on the street. Another shows a crowd of stone-faced unemployed men. One holds a paper announcing a Mayday labor protest.

In a city street scene, people walk apathetically by a major accident on the street, implying citizen's lack of concern for each other during these tough times.

The most cheerful mural presents a panoramic view of California agriculture. Here, at least, the workers are outdoors, collecting bright cut flowers and laying apricots out to dry. Other murals are not entirely humorless. In the mural depicting Banking and Law, take a close look at some of the titles. One reads the <u>Laws of Fresco Painting</u>.

An old-fashioned elevator and a narrow spiral staircase takes you up to the very tip of 180-foot Coit Tower. Here you can enjoy a panoramic view of San Francisco. Far below, you'll see the 12-foot bronze statue of Christopher Columbus gazing over the waters of the Bay.

Coit Tower
Telegraph Hill, San Francisco
415/274-0203
Open daily 10-5 March-Sept., 9-4 Oct.-Feb.
$3 Adults; $2 Seniors 64 and over; $1 ages 6-12

de Young Museum

The de Young is more than a fine art museum. It is a walk through our nation's history and culture. From the austere 17th-century "Mason Children" to 20th-century realist William Glackens' rambunctious working class picnic scene, the collection illustrates our heritage in a new light--through art.

The best way to see the de Young is to join a free guided tour. Several are offered each day, focusing on different aspects of the museum. The enthusiastic, informative docents tell the story behind the artwork and point out details usually overlooked. Each tour is unique.

The de Young's masterworks include portraits by Copley, Sargent, Whistler and Mary Cassatt. There are landscapes by Bierstadt and Frederic Church. Trompe l'oeil paintings include William Harnett's "After the Hunt" and Alexander Pope's "The Trumpeter Swan." You'll see sculptures by Frederic Remington and William Story, silver by Paul Revere, furniture by Stickley and much more. Some of these may be covered on your guided tour. Allow time afterwards to see those you missed.

The galleries are arranged chronologically and the works brightly illuminated with the glowing natural light of wall-to-wall skylights.

The 1670 "Mason Children" is one of the few paintings created in the burgeoning colonies. The clothes are simple, but a touch of wealth is shown in the boy's gloves and silver-handled cane. The girl holds a gaudy red necklace, thought to ward off witches. The Salem witch trials took place just 20 years later. This painting was passed down for three centuries through descendents of the girl in the painting.

Across the room is a portrait by John Singleton Copley, considered the first accomplished painter born in America. This 1770s painting of a New England gentleman and his son exhibits more graceful, life-like figures than his 17th-century predecessor. The shoulders of the man's colonial vestments reveal traces of white powder from his powdered wig, that era's fashion statement. The wigs were valued so highly that thieves snatched them off heads of gentlemen on the street.

In the mid-19th century, landscapes came in vogue, to show God's works, not man's. One gallery wall is devoted to Albert Bierstadt, illustrating his entire career. With the westward expansion, people back east were intrigued with scenes from the new frontier. Works here include the 1871-'72 view of Donner Lake, commissioned to show the building of the transcontinental railroad.

The 1895 bronze sculpture "The Bronco Buster" by Frederic Remington shows another side of the west. Both man and horse reveal their fight and fury.

By the early 20th century, artists expanded beyond portraits and landscapes to the heart of their subject. Georgia O'Keefe's 1925 "Petunias" shows the supple, sensuous beauty in a simple flower.

From the Puritans to the free spirits, a tour of American art in the de Young is sure to give you a new understanding of our culture.

The de Young Museum
Golden Gate Park, San Francisco
415/750-3600
Wed.-Sun. 10-5
$5 Adults; $3 Seniors 65 and over; $2 ages 12-17; under 12 free
Includes same-day admission to Asian Art Museum
Free first Sat. morning and first Wed. of each month

Fort Mason Ethnic Museums

What happens when a military base becomes defunct? A small miracle in the case of Fort Mason in San Francisco. Ex-military buildings have been transformed into offices for such cultural organizations as Make-A-Circus, Friends of the River and the National Poetry Association. Best of all, several rooms are now ethnic and folk museums.

Within short walking distance are the San Francisco Craft and Folk Art Museum, the African American Historical & Cultural Society, the Museo ItaloAmericano and the Mexican Museum.

These museums are small but sharply focused. They primarily feature changing exhibits. Call ahead to find out about the current exhibit and to make sure the museum will be open on the day you visit. They sometimes close when setting up a new exhibit.

Each museum also has a gift shop with unique items from their cultural groups, from carved wooden African animals to bright Mexican pottery. You can see just one museum or all of them in an afternoon, then indulge in a goodie from the Tassajara Bakery or Greens vegetarian restaurant.

The San Francisco Craft & Folk Art Museum is devoted to contemporary craft, American folk art and traditional ethnic art. Some exhibits here have travelled as far as New York, Chicago and Washington, DC. You might see a display of hand-painted third world billboards or finely crafted handmade porcelains.

The African American Historical & Cultural Society lends unique insight into traditional tribal lifestyles as well as the histories of local black pioneers. One recent exhibit featured a Maasai lion killer spear and a helmet mask worn by ceremonial dancers in the Sande Society.

The Museo ItaloAmericano showcases contemporary works by Italian artists while the Mexican Museum features changing exhibits by Mexican craftspeople.

One remnant of the fort's military past is anchored in the water and open to the public. The immense Jeremiah O'Brien is the only existing Liberty ship in its original condition. Launched in 1943, it once carried food and ammunition to Britain, transported supplies to the south Pacific and ferried troops and materiel during the Normandy invasion.

Pick up the free, monthly Fort Mason Center tabloid while you're visiting. It lists the many activities and classes, from martial arts to MacIntosh basics, that help make this a thriving cultural enclave.

SF Craft & Folk Art Museum
Bldg. A, Fort Mason, San Francisco
415/775-0990
Tu.-Sun. 11-5
$1 Adults; $.50 Seniors and ages 12-17
Free on Saturdays from 10-Noon
African American Historical Society
Bldg. C, Fort Mason, San Francisco
415/441-0640
Wed.-Sun. 12-5
$1 Adults; $.50 Seniors and Children under 15
Museo ItaloAmericano
Bldg. C, Fort Mason, San Francisco
415/673-2200
Wed.-Sun. 12-5
$2 Adults; $1 Seniors and Students
Mexican Museum
Bldg. D, Fort Mason, San Francisco
415/441-0404
Wed.-Sun. 12-5; first Wed. of each month 12-8
$2 Adults; $1 Seniors and Students
Free first Wed. of each month
Jeremiah O'Brien
Waterfront, Fort Mason, San Francisco
415/441-3101
Open daily 9-3. Closed major holidays.
$2 Adults; $1 over 59 and under 12; $6 family rate

Haas-Lilienthal House

A new popularity in Victoriana has brought about magnificent restorations of San Francisco's Victorian houses. Many are elegant bed and breakfast inns, others elaborate private residences. But the Haas-Lilienthal House is a home where you feel more like an old friend than a tourist.

Generations of the same family have lived in this grand Victorian since it was built in 1886 until it was donated to the Foundation for San Francisco's Architectural Heritage in 1972.

Almost all of the family's furnishings are still here, reflecting the home's Victorian origins as well as the changes that the family had introduced over the years. Family members still return to the home for a celebration every Christmas.

The house was built originally for William Haas, a German native who sought his fortune in the gold mines, but found it in the wholesale grocery business in San Francisco. He married Bertha Greenebaum in 1880 and built this home six years later.

The other half of the house's name comes from their daughter, Alice, and her husband, Samuel Lilienthal. The happy couple was wed in the formal parlor of this home in 1909. After Alice passed on, her heirs donated the house in its remarkably unchanged condition.

From the outside, the Haas-Lilienthal House looks fit for a queen, but this was actually an upper middle class home. In 1886, the family invested $18,000 for the house and $14,000 for the land. At the time, several grand Victorians graced the neighborhood, most of which have fallen beneath the developer's hammer.

This is a fine example of transitional architecture. The rectangular bay windows are Stick Eastlake style, popular in the late 1880s. The gables, varied shingles and graceful round tower reflect the Queen Anne style, which came into vogue in the 1890s.

As you walk through the front door, the house immediately emits a lived-in rather than staid museum feel. The foyer and main hallway are dark by today's standards. Deep green wallpaper is patterned to simulate grained leather highlighted with gold embossing. An intricately detailed grandfather clock comes from the family's native Germany.

As in many Victorian homes, the hallway leads from the front to the back of the house, opening on one side to a formal parlor, center parlor and dining room with 13-foot-high ceilings. Oriental vases decorate the parlor's mantel. Goods from China took a mere six weeks to arrive compared with months for decorative ware from the east coast or Europe.

The dining table could seat 22 people. The hutch's glass-enclosed cabinets still showcase the family's gold-laced stemware. You'll find a 1927 stove and oven in the kitchen, along with the original marble-topped table where the cook could roll out strudel.

A later influence also is found upstairs in the bedroom that Bertha converted to her sitting room. Alice and Samuel's bedroom still has the furniture they received as a wedding gift. It's a twin bed set, but the pattern shows that the beds were meant to be placed together.

In the children's room is a charming white bassinet which is still used by the family when a baby is born. Other delightful furnishings include child-size, fully upholstered Stick Eastlake chairs.

As in other rooms in the house, you almost expect a family member to come in at any moment and offer you a cup of tea.

Haas-Lilienthal House
2007 Franklin St. (at Washington), San Francisco
415/441-3004
Tours Wed. 11:30-3:30, Sun. Noon-4
$4 Adults; $2 Seniors over 65 and Children under 12

North Beach

Caffe Roma, Biordi Art, Stella Pastry, Bocce Cafe, Panelli Deli, Fior d'Italia. The names of North Beach bring back the old country, a slice of Italy right in the hub of San Francisco. And if the names don't transport you to Europe, the sights, sounds, delicious tastes and scents will.

Washington Square is the soul of North Beach and the best place to begin a walk around our city's "Little Italy." Now landlocked, the name "North Beach" dates to the 1850s when a finger of the Bay extended here. If you come early in the morning, you'll see dozens of Chinese men and women performing the slow stretches of T'ai Chi on the soft grasses of the Square. Once exclusively Italian, North Beach has become a cultural melting pot, with Chinese, Basque, Persian and even Tunisian restaurants among the Italian cafes.

The Romanesque, cathedral-style Church of Saints Peter and Paul, completed in 1924, reigns over Washington Square. Its twin spires soar 191 feet high, flanking a 14-foot-wide rosette window and a large arched doorway. Inside, glowing white and intricately carved statues, domes and spires rise above the main altar of Carrara marble. Candles flicker in the shrines. Mosaics line the walls.

From the church, cross the square and walk up Columbus Avenue. Small Italian, family-owned shoe-shine shops, delis and cafes line the street.

Coffee lovers shouldn't miss the Caffe Roma Coffee Roasting Company at 526 Columbus. Dominating the shop is the immense, sparkling brass and burgundy machine that roasts beans fresh on the spot, creating that heavenly aroma. Enthusiastic owner Tony Azzollini studied with the roasting maestros in Italy and he's happy to show you how he creates his own perfect blend.

Indulge in a sweet cookie or cake at Stella Pastry at 446 Columbus. Look in their inviting display case to find Amaretti and Pignolati cookies, Napoleons, Sacripantina and Tirami Su cakes. At 412 Columbus, browse through Biordi Art Imports' collection of stunning Majolica pottery. These are classic, intricately hand-painted patterns, many from the town of Deruta, Italy's largest pottery center.

The North Beach Museum, on the mezzanine of the EurekaBank at 1435 Stockton, illustrates the far-reaching influence of the neighborhood's Italian and Chinese residents on the burgeoning city.

For more than 40 years, curator Alessandro Baccari has collected historical photographs, family heirlooms and vintage books to tell their story. You'll discover that the Bank of America began as the Bank of Italy. You'll realize that it's no coincidence Italian names reign over seafood restaurants on the wharf. You'll know why the Chinese choose Washington Square for T'ai Chi.

The first Italians immigrated here in the 1840s to a small village named Yerba Buena. But the discovery of gold in 1848 created an overnight boomtown and it was renamed San Francisco. By the 1880s, North Beach was predominantly Italian. Many worked as fishermen and produce farmers.

The museum's exhibits change periodically, but generally focus on the family life of North Beach. Among the heirlooms is a complete 1870s table setting with china, silverware, wineglasses and candlesticks. The richly embroidered priest's vestments were presented to Baccari's great, great uncle by the devoted parishioners of Saints Peter and Paul in 1917. Chinese residents have donated Chinese books used in San Francisco schools. Historical photographs set the scene.

Despite its compact size, the North Beach museum presents an intriguing, new perspective on the family life, history and cultural heritage of San Francisco's "Little Italy."

North Beach Museum
EurekaBank, 1435 Stockton St,. San Francisco
415/391-6210
Mon.-Th. 9-3:30; Fri. 9-4
Free

☼ Old Mint &
Ansel Adams Center

It's like an Egyptian tomb, dark and mysterious at first, then alight with the glitter of gold. Twenty-eight gold bars, worth about $150,000 each, are stacked in a pyramid and surrounded by an overflowing pile of antique gold coins and several pieces of natural gold leaf. All together, this collection is worth more than $4 million.

This is the original gold deposit vault at the Old Mint in San Francisco. This massive, Greek Revival building is a treasure trove not only of gold, but of California history and our nation's numismatics. Gleaming proof sets of coins and century-old mint machinery are sure to give you a new appreciation for the change in your pocket.

Opened in 1874 to accommodate the influx of gold from the Mother Lode and San Francisco's booming financial market, the Mint was constructed to withstand earthquakes and fires. It proved its mettle in 1906, when it stood unscathed while the city collapsed and burned around it.

With brick and stone walls, a granite floor and interior cast iron columns supporting a cast iron ceiling, the Mint is as solid today as ever. Although everyday coins are no longer produced here, you can still stamp out your own commemorative medal on the circa-1869, 160-ton press for $1.

Commemorative medals, honoring presidents, historic anniversaries and statesmen, are big business with collectors. The Old Mint's gift shop offers a fine selection of them. These, along with proof sets of everyday coins, are produced in the new San Francisco Mint, located a short distance away.

Coins are miniature works of art when produced as proof sets. Each cent, nickel, dime and quarter is painstakingly created by hand. First, the dies, which stamp the picture onto the coin blank, are polished with several grades of diamond polish, then buffed.

Coin blanks are burnished with thousands of steel beads and cleaning chemicals before being sent to the press. The combination of custom-made dies and blanks results in gleaming, high-relief coins worth several times their face value.

Only one-quarter of the building is devoted to museum space, but there's plenty to see. One room recreates a Victorian bedchamber, another the Superintendent's Office with original furnishings from 1874. Memorabilia, including typewriters, Victrolas and quilts, are part of their collection.

A beautiful six-foot scale, with gold leaf highlights and ivory handles, stands in the hallway. Scales of this type still are used to weigh bags of coins in the new mint.

The Ansel Adams Center is a short walk away. It's run by the Friends of Photography, founded 24 years ago in Carmel and now one of the oldest photography organizations in the world. The museum encompasses several galleries, one devoted to Adams prints. Others showcase changing exhibits of major photographers and young, emerging artists.

Adams is best known for his black-and-white nature shots. The play of light and shadow in Yosemite was one of his favorite subjects. His images of Half Dome and Yosemite Valley are two of the most widely recognized photographs in the world. A staunch conservationist, Adams' photographs were not only works of art, but a call to preserve America's wilderness.

The Old Mint
Fifth and Mission, San Francisco
415/744-6830
Mon.-Fri. 10-4; Tours every hour on the half-hour
Free
Ansel Adams Center
250 Fourth St., San Francisco
415/495-7000
Tues.-Sun. 11-6
$4 Adults; $3 Students with ID;
$2 Seniors 65 and over and ages 12-17

Rodin Sculpture Garden

The second largest collection of Rodin sculptures in the world is not in the museum of a great metropolis. It belongs to Stanford University. The collection encompasses 125 of Rodin's masterpieces. Several, including "The Thinker," are found throughout the campus, but the best place to see the sculptor's work is in the Rodin Sculpture Garden next to the Stanford Museum.

The garden design is simple, an open, quiet setting for the 20 bronze sculptures exhibited here. The pieces have been placed to receive the maximum benefit from sunlight, which accentuates the figures' fluid lines and facial expressions.

Auguste Rodin (1840-1917) was a master sculptor from a small town outside Paris. He created his figures in clay, then crafted plaster molds for the bronze casting. The sculptures in this garden are authentic and original, but not unique. They are cast in molds that Rodin created.

Rodin wanted his sculptures to be distributed around the world. His will authorized the French government to cast with his molds after his death, but this has been strictly controlled with limited editions.

The most intricate work in this garden is The Gates of Hell. It is a provoking, nightmarish vision of Pandemonium. Two massive bronze doors are alive with anguished men and women struggling to escape the flames.

Many of the figures are not much larger than a human hand, yet each features a unique expression of anguish and fear as they plummet downward. Above the gates is a small-scale figure of The Thinker. On either side, life-size figures of Adam and Eve turn away from the searing heat of the flames.

Rodin worked on The Gates of Hell on and off for 20 years. Since the first bronze castings weren't made until the 1920s, he never saw the finished masterpiece cast in bronze.

There are only five castings of The Gates of Hell in the world today: in Paris, Philadelphia, Tokyo, Zurich and right here at Stanford. The Stanford piece took over four years to cast, from 1977 to 1981. It is the fifth and last cast made of The Gates of Hell, cast using the lost wax method.

While working on The Gates of Hell, Rodin enlarged some of the figures to exhibit as sculptures in their own right. These are found in the East Court of Stanford's Rodin sculpture garden. The South Court focuses on Rodin's monuments and tributes to artists.

The boundaries of the Terrace trace the foundations of the wings of the Stanford Museum lost in the 1906 earthquake. On the Western Terrace are the partial figures of Rodin's famous Burghers of Calais. Four more full-size figures from the Burghers stand in Stanford's quad, a short walk away.

Just beyond is Memorial Church, one of the most beautiful buildings on campus. This is the centerpiece of the Main Quadrangle, Stanford's first buildings. The front facade of the church frames a sparkling gold mural of "Christ welcoming the righteous into heaven." It is a striking contrast to Rodin's tormented Gates of Hell.

Rodin Sculpture Garden
Stanford University
415/723-3469
Garden open 24 hours daily
Tours offered Wed., Sat. & Sun. 2:00
Free

Rosicrucian Egyptian Museum

The dim beam of the guide's flashlight leads the way through the dark and narrow hallways of the tomb to the room holding the sarcophagus. It flashes on colorful wall paintings depicting everyday life of the dead noble's estate. On the rock ceiling above the sarcophagus, an immense, gracefully serene image of a goddess has been painted to protect the deceased from grave robbers. It didn't work. A corner of the sarcophagus has been hacked out and valuables stolen.

This is one of the unusual highlights of the Rosicrucian Egyptian Museum in San Jose, which is devoted to artifacts of the ancient world. The tomb is a life-size composite replica of Egyptian rock tombs from 4,000 years in the past. The building of these grand structures sometimes began at the noble's birth. Wall paintings of bakers, fishermen and cattle being led to market bring back the times of the deceased. Some sketches have not been colored in yet. The noble died before the tomb could be completed.

Many more cedar sarcophagi and mummies are displayed in the museum's exhibit rooms. Although thousands of years old, they are still nearly perfectly preserved. On some mummies, like Usermontu, a priest buried in Thebes in 630 BC, you can still distinguish the man's facial characteristics and see his fingernails and toenails. Animals also were mummified, including a baboon, from about 525 BC and a gazelle, from 1400 BC. Three cat mummies represent hundreds found. Cats were sacred to Bast, one of the more popular goddesses

Writing, in the form of hieroglyphics, is one of the most important legacies of the ancient world. A replica of the Rosetta Stone is on display. The original was found in 1799 near the Nile. Since it was written in both Egyptian hieroglyphics and Greek, it was key to understanding Egyptian history and culture.

Scribes were considered some of society's most important members. Their work is exhibited on the dozens of clay tablets, some no bigger than your palm, that fill the museum's display cases. Many of these are religious writings, invoices, receipts and medical texts from 2800 to 200 BC.

Babylonian businessmen dictated messages which a scribe engraved onto a wet clay tablet. After authenticating the written message with the businessman's stamp, the tablet was dusted with a fine powder, then sealed in a clay "envelope." It was addressed by the scribe and baked to harden. A Pony Express-style system delivered the package to its recipient who cracked open the envelope to retrieve the message.

Ancient musical instruments reveal another lifestyle of the ancients. Ivory castanets in the shape of two hands date to 1400 BC. A bronze sistrum, shaken like a noisemaker, was used in temples for the adoration of Isis and became the symbol for cosmic motion. Present-day priests still believe the rattling sound drives away evil spirits.

Plan to spend some time exploring the park surrounding the museum as well. Its Egyptian-style buildings, verdant lawns, obelisk and statuary make a peaceful sanctuary to ponder the ancient world.

The Rosicrucian Egyptian Museum
Corner of Park and Naglee Avenues, San Jose
408/287-2807
Daily 9-5
$4 Adults; $3.50 Seniors 65 and over
& Students with ID; $2 ages 7-15
Free Sat. & Sun. 9 A.M.-11 A.M.

Extra Tip...Save 50% off each adult admission. See Bonus Coupon Section.

Behring Auto Museum

Before the assembly line robot came the artist. This simple fact inspired real estate magnate Ken Behring to create a collection of classic cars which is one of the finest of its kind in the world.

These are the crown jewels of their era--the customized Packards, Cadillacs and one-of-a-kind sports cars. Like jewels, they are displayed in a magnificent setting--the opulent Behring Auto Museum in Blackhawk Plaza.

A gilded gate and low rising stairs past fountains and waterfalls lead to the museum's faceted smoked glass facade. Inside, two showrooms house more than 100 automotive masterpieces. Subdued lighting and classical music set the tone. Spotlights highlight the ruby, sapphire, silver and gold colors of the cars.

The collection, valued at $100 million, includes some of the rarest cars on Earth. Signs point out unique design details, outline outstanding engine performance or relate fascinating historical facts. Some cars belonged to Hollywood celebrities. Others were custom-made for royalty.

The first floor gallery is arranged chronologically, a walk through automotive history. It begins with an 1897 three-wheel Leon Bollee Voiturette. The 1901 Oldsmobile curved dash runabout was one of America's first production cars. With seven horsepower, it could reach 20 mph.

One corner is devoted to race cars, from the 1912 Stutz Bearcat Series A to the 1975 McLaren race car in which Johnny Rutherford won the 1976 Indy 500. The 1917 Hudson Super-six two-seater is the first and only Hudson to race in the Indy 500. There were no pit stops in those days. The extra seat was for the mechanic.

By the 1930s, automobiles began to shape society. The green and yellow 1930 Lincoln Model

L-77 Sport Touring car was favored by police and gangsters. It was fast, roomy and rugged.

One-of-a-kind cars include the 1941 Lincoln Continental by industrial designer Raymond Loewy, one of only two ever built. Loewy is known for designing the Shell Oil logo, Frigidaire appliances and Studebakers. The lines in this deep green car are nearly as fluid as water.

Video displays tell the story of three famous automobile designers, including Frank Hershey. He introduced the fins of the '50s, shown to their height in several models displayed in this museum.

The 1957 Cadillac Eldorado Brougham, with its brushed stainless steel roof, was the most expensive production car Cadillac ever built. Little luxuries included a cigarette case, tissue dispenser, vanity compact, magnetized cups and perfume atomizer.

The sporty, red 1965 Chevrolet Corvette Stingray Coupe is one of the best restored of its kind in the world.

The third floor showcases unique automobiles with fascinating histories. The sleek 1924 Hispano-Suiza race car has a body of ribbed, finely rubbed tulip wood, with copper rivets and wheels.

The most extravagant car is the 1926 Daimler Salon Cabriolet, custom built for the Maharaja of Rewa's tiger hunts. Its nickel silver body has horns in the form of snakes rising over the front wheels and a hood ornament resembling a Grecian bust.

The 1956 red Jaguar was owned by actor Ricardo Montalban. Comedienne Lucille Ball cruised Hollywood streets in the silvery blue 1962 Dual-Ghia coupe. Clark Gable courted Carole Lombard in the 1935 lemon yellow Duesenberg convertible. Who could resist?

Behring Auto Museum
Camino Tassajara and Blackhawk Rd., Blackhawk
Exit I-680 in Danville at Sycamore Valley Rd.
Head east 4 1/2 miles. Museum on left.
510/736-2277 (recording)
Open Tu.-Sun. 10-5; Wed. & Fri. until 9 PM
$5 Adults; $3 Seniors (65 and over) and ages 6-17

Judah L. Magnes Museum

Housed in a 1908 mansion on one of Berkeley's prettiest streets, the Magnes is the third largest Jewish museum in the United States. Its permanent collection encompasses 10,000 objects. Its Judaica Library contains 10,000 volumes. Its Western Jewish History Center includes 20,000 items.

The museum's "Holiday Room" is an intriguing place to start discovering the basics of Chanukah and other Jewish celebrations.

Illustrating a calendar year of Jewish holidays, the exhibits contain objects found in Jewish homes as well as synagogues. Jewish ceremonies are very home-oriented.

In the Sabbath display case are Kiddush goblets, Challah knives for cutting braided egg bread and intricate silver spice boxes. The Kiddush is the blessing said over the wine. Another blessing is said while cutting with the Challah knife.

The spice box contains cinnamon, cloves or nutmeg, so the sweetness of the Sabbath can linger throughout the week. The spice boxes displayed here are intricately crafted silver, mostly from 19th-century Russia and Germany. One resembles a castle's turret with waving flags.

Sabbath objects like these are used today in many Jewish homes. An interesting assortment of spice boxes is available at the museum's gift shop.

The Chanukah exhibit illustrates the extraordinary diversity of Chanukah lamps. Some are the familiar Menorah-style, a candelabra with eight curved arms. Many show the influence of different cultures on the religion. A 14th-century Chanukah lamp from Spain has a cut-out rose window above a colonnade of Moorish arches. One from 19th-century Iran is a flat brass sheet that looks like a pavilion with two small side towers.

Chanukah is a historic holiday, not actually mentioned in the Torah, that celebrates a resistance movement at the end of Alexander's empire, about 165 B.C. When Jewish freedom fighters recaptured and rededicated their synagogue, the perpetual light had enough oil to burn only one more day. The light is never supposed to burn out, but it would take eight days to create more lamp oil. Miraculously, the perpetual light continued to burn for those eight days.

This event is just one of the cycles when Jews were persecuted then rose again. The museum's "Room of Remembrance" illustrates other eras of anti-Semitism. Most prominent are objects from Nazi Germany. One case displays a burnt Torah scroll from Kristalnacht. The Torah scroll, containing the Holy Word, is the Jew's most sacred object, to be treated with the utmost reverence. Another display shows a defiled segment of Torah scroll used as a canvas for an oil painting.

One of the Magnes' missions is to preserve Jewish artifacts; many were lost during times of anti-Semitism. In the upstairs hall is a large stained glass window representing the 12 tribes of Israel, probably from a synagogue. Someone found it in an antique store. The Torah and Synagogue Room contains artifacts spanning five centuries and objects from around the world.

In addition to the permanent collection, the museum's temporary exhibits celebrate works by contemporary Jewish artists, art with Jewish themes and Jewish lifestyles in other cultures.

After touring the museum, you can relax in the picnic area, surrounded by roses and palms in a garden designed by John McLaren, the landscape architect for Golden Gate Park.

Judah L. Magnes Museum
2911 Russell St., Berkeley
501/849-2710
Sun. - Th. 10-4; Tours offered Sun. & Wed.
$3 Donation suggested

Mormon Temple

You can see it from the freeway, a glowing white monument high in the Oakland hills. Ships and planes use it as a landmark. Visitors from around the world are attracted to it like a beacon.

Next time you have an hour to spare, satisfy your curiosity and drive up to the Oakland Temple of the Church of Jesus Christ of Latter-day Saints. Members of the Mormon Church will be on hand to show you around this inspiring setting and explain the basics of their religious beliefs.

The gleaming white granite Temple follows an Oriental motif, with five pinnacle spires reaching heavenward. A long walkway lined with colorful flowers, tumbling waterfalls and splashing fountains draws the eye to this most sacred of the Mormons' meeting places. Beyond is a cloud-high view of Oakland, the Bay and the San Francisco skyline on the horizon. The sweet scent of flowers and piped-in music of the Mormon Tabernacle Choir enhance the site's peaceful aura.

You begin your tour at the Visitor Center, where you can pick up brochures on the Church's history and choose from a list of 20 to 30-minute films to watch. Rather than preaching, the films focus on common sense questions, such as the purpose of life, and illustrate them with everyday, feel-good people and stories. As the tour guide will tell you, they're not trying to convince you but simply want to share what they've found.

The architecturally unique Temple is the beacon that draws people from the freeway, but don't expect to see its interior. Because it is sacred, only Church members in good standing are allowed to enter. Even then members only use the Temple for four highly sacred purposes: marriage, certain baptisms, a "sealing" ceremony to unite families and certain promises with God.

Regular Sunday meetings are held in the Inter-Stake Center, the long building next to the Temple, which is open to the public. This Center encompasses 170 rooms, with two gymnasiums, three chapels, two kitchens, a 2,000-seat auditorium and its well-used genealogical library.

In the chapels, Sunday sacrament meetings are conducted in a variety of languages, including Tongan, Samoan, Vietnamese, Chinese, Spanish and English. The auditorium's highlight is the immense organ with more than 4,500 pipes.

Have you ever wondered where your ancestors were during the Renaissance? The most popular room in the Center is the genealogical library, a branch of the world-renowned library in Salt Lake City. About 80% of its users are non-Mormons who are researching family trees. Volunteers and a short film will show you how to get started.

Even the non-religious will find it's well worth the trip to the Church of Jesus Christ of Latter-day Saints to see the architecture, to study in the genealogical library and to learn more about the religion of the Mormons.

While you're in the area, visit Joaquin Miller Park, a short drive east of the Temple off Joaquin Miller Road. Miller was an Indian fighter, pony express rider, judge, gold prospector and writer, but he is best known for his trees. He and his friends planted 75,000 of them--Monterey pines, cypress, and, reportedly, California's first eucalyptus.

Today, you can hike in this 500-acre forest park and visit the stone monuments that Miller erected to those he most admired, such as poets Robert and Elizabeth Browning and Moses. Bring a picnic to enjoy at the shaded sites overlooking panoramic views of San Francisco.

Oakland Temple of the Church
of Jesus Christ of Latter-day Saints
4770 Lincoln Ave., Oakland
510/531-1475
Guided tours daily 9-9
Free

Marin County Civic Center

When most people think "government building," they think drab, gray and institutional. But the Marin County Civic Center in San Rafael is bright, creative and uplifting. It is a flowing sculpture, thanks to the genius of a master architect, Frank Lloyd Wright.

For anyone who equates touring a government building with watching the paint dry, a visit here is an eye-opening experience. Enthusiastic docents lead individuals and groups through the structure to a better understanding of what architecture can be in the hands of a visionary like Wright.

In 1957, when Wright was 90 years old, he stood on the hill outside what is now the fourth floor and said he was going to create a building "that would undulate like a caterpillar over the hills of Marin."

In keeping with Wright's Taliesin principle, he designed a low-lying building that would flow with the land rather than fight against it. All together, the civic center stretches over 1,300 feet, almost five football fields long. It's been compared to a 10-story skyscraper, but on its side. Like a sculpture, a single vertical accents the structure, the pagoda-style peak that masks the building's exhaust system.

Once inside, the low-rising stairs to the first floor are a Wright trademark, so the visitor would enter slowly and deliberately and the building would unfold before you. The escalator to the second floor has the same effect as the arched skylights above are gradually revealed.

The upper floors follow Wright's classic "destruction of the box." The space is open, airy and bright, with flowing, rounded lines. Offices are on the outer perimeters of the building. The center is an elongated oval atrium, rising three stories to the skylights. Each floor's oval opening is graduated, so the upper balcony will not shadow the sun lighting the lower balconies. This design achieves Wright's goal to bring the outdoors in and the indoors out.

Although one of his students, Aaron Greene, took on the interior design after Wright's death in 1958, Wright's concept is carried through to the last detail. The circular motif is found in the drinking fountains, door handles and benches. Greene described the spheres trimming the walls as "a string of pearls on a black dress."

In his building for democracy, Wright believed that citizens should be able to see their government in action. As you walk down the hall, you can look into the windows of each office.

The round library is in the center of the structure. In the circular courtrooms, the walnut panels are handrubbed and taken from the same tree to ensure a fluid look.

Downstairs, a display case holds Wright's original model for the civic center. He envisioned a much longer building. What was to be the Health and Human Services department is now a garage. The grand arch at the entrance to the Civic Center complex never materialized. Still, the structure is pure Frank Lloyd Wright.

In keeping with the theme of bringing the outdoors in and indoors out, the civic center's cafeteria opens onto a delightful courtyard, with round patio stones and a circular pond. It is a sunny vantage point to view this entire sculpture of a building.

Marin County Civic Center
N. San Pedro exit off 101 North, San Rafael
415/499-7407
Tours offered Mon.-Fri. 9-3:30;
One week advance notice requested
Free

Crocker Art Museum

The Crocker Art Museum is the oldest public art museum in the west. Housed in an Italianate Victorian mansion, the building, itself, is a masterpiece. Built in 1871 for Judge Edwin Crocker and his family, it served not only as their home, but also as an enviable entertainment center and art gallery. The mansion once boasted a bowling alley, skating rink, billiard room, elaborate ballroom and library.

While it was being built, the Crockers enjoyed a grand tour of Europe, collecting old masters to display in their new home. Many of the oils exhibited today are the works that the Crockers originally purchased. Crocker also acquired a worthy collection of paintings by the California artists of his time, including such greats as Thomas Hill, William Keith and Charles Christian Nahl.

No expense was spared in decorating the floors, walls and ceiling during the Victorians' elaborate heyday. Every detail has been restored to reflect its original appearance. You walk through immense carved wooden doors to an entryway with an ornate but tasteful tile floor and intricately painted ceiling. Curved staircases rise up either side to the European and California galleries.

In the European Hall, you'll find the rich colors and dramatic figures of 16th-century Flemish works and 17th-century Dutch and Italian paintings. Many depict Biblical or mythical scenes.

One of the grandest works in the Early California Hall is Thomas Hill's "Great Canyons of the Sierra--Yosemite," painted in 1871. It measures 6 by 10 feet. Light appears to glow on the cliffs, with a waterfall feathering into the valley and Half Dome looming in the background. Another landscape by

William Keith shows what Mt. Tamalpais looked like in 1871.

On the first level, the Crockers' magnificent ballroom nearly overwhelms the artworks displayed. It features parquet floors, rich wood wainscotting and an intricately painted ceiling. Stand beneath the second chandelier and look up. You will see a patch of the original design exposed to show how closely the restoration matches.

A period room recreates the Crocker family parlor from 1870 through 1885. Furnishings include a rococo mirrored etagere with shelves for displaying yet more porcelain artworks. This room saw the wedding of Katie Crocker in February of 1874 and her funeral in October of that year.

The Crockers acquired 150 contemporary German paintings during their European travels in the early 1870s. These now comprise one of the largest collections of German popular art in the U.S. Many are scenes of the everyday life of the common man and are enhanced by excellent signs describing the paintings.

You'll also find contemporary works at the Crocker and fine special exhibits at any time of year. Just six blocks from the heart of Old Sacramento, the Crocker is a don't miss for anyone touring the area.

Crocker Art Museum
3rd and O Sts., Sacramento
916/449-5423
Wed.-Sun. 10-5, Th. 10-9
$3 Adults; $1.50 ages 7-17

Extra Tip...Get one free admission with one paid admission. See Bonus Coupon Section.

Extra, Extra Tip...If you're planning to see several Sacramento sites, invest in a Joint Admission Ticket. Good for one year, it covers admission to the Crocker Art Museum, California State Railroad Museum, Central Pacific Railroad Depot, Sacramento History Center, Sutter's Fort, Indian Museum and Governor's Mansion. It costs $11 Adults and $5 for ages 6-12.

Towe Ford Museum

The "World's Most Complete Antique Ford Museum" isn't in Michigan. It's right here in Sacramento. More than 170 automobiles, from a 1903 Model A to a sporty 'sixties Mustang, fill this cavernous garage.

The cars are arranged chronologically. Walking through the museum is like walking through 20th-century American history and rediscovering the automobile's distinctive role in that history.

Period music from the various decades plays in the background. Displays list world events of selected production years to bring back the times of the cars' original owners. A few artifacts, such as vintage clothing and advertisements, personalize the machines. You can even climb inside and sit behind the steering wheel of a Model T.

From 1912 until 1924, Henry Ford was responsible for manufacturing half of all motorcars in use in the United States. It began in 1896 in his Detroit workshop. Ford pieced together bicycle chains, wheels and other parts to a buggy frame and attached a gasoline-powered engine. The first Model A, displayed in the museum, isn't much more than a modified horse carriage with brass headlights and a wood steering wheel.

You can see how the automobile evolved as you walk past the early cars. Almost every year and model produced by Ford in its first 50 years is on display. By the time the Model T was introduced, Ford was unable to manufacture enough cars to meet demand, despite his pioneering mass production methods that turned out 15 million Model Ts from 1908 to 1927.

Individuals customized Fords to their personal needs, as in the 1929 Model A mail truck and 1930 red Model AA dump truck. One rare adaptation is the 1931 Model A produce truck used in Hawaii to ship fruit around the island. The chassis, frame and engine were shipped to Hawaii, where a custom truck body was added. Only 25 of these were made. This is the only surviving "Banana Wagon."

One scene is straight out of <u>Grapes of Wrath</u>. A 1917 Model T truck is loaded with such depression-era goods as a disassembled windmill and prized mirror. A simple camp, with a coffeepot over a campfire, stools and a wash basin, sets in front--a typical scene along Route 66 as families headed to California.

Another scene embodies the World War II era. Period music, newspaper headlines proclaiming the Pearl Harbor bombing and a collection of gas ration coupons form the backdrop for a 1943 Ford jeep with Army markings. The jeep is the "grandfather" of today's 4-wheel drive vehicles.

Roomy sedans from the 1950s are parked as though they're at a drive-in movie, with speakers attached to their windows. An enviable 1957 Skyliner convertible features a retractable hardtop that folded back into the car's trunk.

A 1964 1/2 Mustang and sleek 1955 Thunderbird are the stars of the southern California beach scene, complete with hamburger stand and surf shop.

Specialized non-Ford automobiles round out the collection, including Governor Jerry Brown's 1974 gas-guzzling blue Plymouth and a 1976 Cadillac armored limousine. Once used by the secret service, the door is open to reveal the nearly 2-inch thick window. Even though it weighed five tons, the limousine could top 80 mph on four flat tires.

Towe Ford Museum
2200 Front St., Sacramento
916/442-6802
Open daily 10-6
$5 Adults; $4.50 Seniors;
$2 High School; $1 Grade School

Extra Tip...Save $1 off adult admission. See Bonus Coupon Section.

Notes

Towns
to
Explore

Half Moon Bay

"You're only 25 miles south of San Francisco, but you're a world away," a Half Moon Bay resident sighed. This quiet coastal village is brimming with old-fashioned charm. You can browse through the fun shops of the quaint downtown, peak into a garden, picnic on the beach or visit a winery.

Half Moon Bay was founded in the 1860s by Portuguese and Italian farmers and fishermen. Today, fishing and agriculture remain two of the area's main industries. The foggy, coastal climate is ideal for growing Brussels sprouts, cut flowers and its most famous produce--pumpkins.

Each autumn, the hills turn orange with a plethora of pumpkins. It's hard to dispute the town's claim that it is the "Pumpkin Capital of the World." Begun in 1970, the annual Half Moon Bay Art & Pumpkin Festival, held the weekend after the Columbus Day observance, now draws about 300,000 people to this tiny town.

Another popular festival is Chamarita, usually held the seventh Sunday after Easter. Chamarita is a holiday of thanksgiving dating back to Queen Isabel of Portugal. It has been celebrated for over a century in Half Moon Bay. A Catholic Mass, parade, carnival and sumptuous barbecue are part of the festivities.

The area's bounty of beautiful bouquet flowers also is celebrated. On the third Saturday of each month from May through September, local floriculture wholesalers set up colorful booths downtown to sell flowers and house plants.

At any time of year, you can see one of the town's prettiest and most accessible gardens by peeking over the fence at Mill Rose Inn, on Mill Street a half-block off Main. Innkeepers Eve and Terry Baldwin, both with degrees in horticulture, have created an explosion of color, with more than 200 varieties of roses, lilies, sweet peas, daisies,

Iceland poppies, irises, delphiniums, lobelia and English lavender.

Up on Half Moon Bay's eclectic Main Street, an art gallery and auto parts store may be next-door neighbors. Cavanaugh Gallery specializes in handcrafted American furnishings and folk art, including rag rugs, tole-painted dressers, upholstered double rockers, whimsical cow planters and wood chairs custom-made by the Amish.

Coastside Books offers a beautiful selection of titles on wildflowers, gardening and aroma therapy. Brightly colored children's clothes fill the racks of P. Cottontail. Take a one-block detour down Miramontes Street to the Community United Methodist Church, built in 1872. Look closely and you'll notice an unusual theme in one of the stained glass windows--pumpkins.

Further down Main street, the Gingerbread Barn is a cozy collection of American folk arts with teddy bears in pinafores, Lizzi High dolls, Wyoming jams and Hawaiian salad dressings. Across the street is the Old Thyme Inn, a restored Victorian bed and breakfast with its own sweet-scented herb garden.

For a touch of old-fashioned Half Moon Bay, drop by Cunha's Country Store. The shop's been open for 100 years and run by the same family for 65 years. Upstairs is a regular emporium of kitchen gadgets, mixing bowls, plaid shirts, bandanas, straw cowboy hats, jeans, fancy cowboy boots, muffin tins, placemats, wrapping paper and much more. Downstairs is a grocery where you can buy local produce and a sandwich for a picnic. Top it off with cookies from the HMB Bakery next door.

Before taking the short drive to the coast's sandy beaches, you may want to detour to Obester Winery, about 2 miles east of town on Highway 92. It's open daily for tasting and sales from 10 to 5 (tel. 415/726-9463).

Half Moon Bay
Chamber of Commerce
225 S. Cabrillo Hwy, Box 188
Half Moon Bay 94019
415/726-5202

Gilroy & Environs

Welcome to "the only town in America where you can marinate a steak by hanging it on the clothesline," according to humorist Will Rogers. Just roll down your car windows and you'll know when you've arrived at Gilroy, the self-proclaimed "Garlic Capital of the World."

This area grows and processes 90% of all the garlic consumed in the United States. Each year, the Gilroy Garlic Festival in late July draws about 140,000 people to this small town. They eat 5,000 pounds of garlic, 19,998 garlic rolls and 15,500 pounds of garlic-laced pepper steak sandwiches. But there's much more to Gilroy than garlic.

Take a quick tour of the town's historic district to see what Main Street, U.S.A. looked like in the 1920s. Monterey Street, between 4th and 6th Streets, is lined with the brick and concrete shops of a working man's downtown.

Head up 1st Street towards the Hecker Pass for one of the most interesting drives in the area. You can't miss the stunning, colorful flower fields and greenhouses of Goldsmith Seeds, the second largest flower seed producer in the world. You're welcome to walk among the rows of well-marked petunias, marigolds and other blooms growing out front.

Within a short distance, you can visit seven wineries, small, family-owned operations run by the same families for generations. The owner may be the one to pour your samples. Surprisingly, this is one of California's oldest wine grape growing regions. The Franciscan fathers first planted vineyards here in the mid-1770s.

After visiting Hecker Pass Winery, the last on this route, double back and take a left on Watsonville Road. You will pass three more wineries, including historic Kirigin vineyards, before circling back to Monterey Street.

Just outside of town (Leavesley Road exit off 101), the Pacific West Outlet Center is a bargain-hunter's paradise of close to 60 factory direct discount stores. Liz Claiborne, Anne Klein and Capezio are some of the brand-name outlets here.

Next, drive further south on 101 to San Juan Bautista. Its 1803 mission has been restored. It offers a cool retreat into history on a hot summer day. Once known as "the Mission of Music," one room contains an old bass, two violins and choir books. A tall music stand features a box from which white doves were released during mass on Pentecost. (Open daily 9:30-5, $1 donation suggested, tel. 408/623-4528)

The State Historic Park preserves the San Juan Bautista of the 1860s and '70s, encompassing nine buildings along with courtyards and gardens. The 1840 Castro House is traditional Spanish architecture, with red-tile roof and a shaded balcony running the length of the adobe structure. Inside, it's furnished in the style of the 1870s. Across the street, the Plaza Stable houses an extensive selection of restored horse-drawn vehicles, from a Parisian coach to a 12-barrel beer wagon. (Park open daily 10-4:30, $2 Adults, $1 ages 6-17, tel. 408/623-4881) Fun handcraft shops, boutiques and restaurants entice visitors to the town's small but diverse main street.

A bit further afield, but well worth the drive for outdoor enthusiasts, is Pinnacles National Monument. You can hike up, around, above and beneath the odd-shaped rock towers that gave the park its name. Tarantulas, wild pigs and neon-colored rock climbers are some of the strange creatures you might encounter here. For more on Pinnacles, see The Great Outdoors chapter.

Gilroy & Environs
Gilroy Visitor's Bureau
7780 Monterey St., Gilroy, CA 95020
408/842-6436

Monterey

Most people visiting Monterey head for the same attractions: Cannery Row, the Aquarium and Fisherman's Wharf. Next time, take a detour.

Follow the Path of History to discover a side of Monterey that many miss--the surprising story of California's first capital. Pick up a map at the Custom House. The Path wends past one of the states' most extensive collections of adobe homes and California's first brick house, first theater, first glass windows and the building where the state's first Constitution was written.

The Custom House is just across from Fisherman's Wharf. This is the oldest government building on the west coast. In the 1820s, Monterey, then under Mexican rule, was California's chief port of entry. Each ship that harbored here had to unload their cargo for inspection and taxation. Inside the Custom House, you will find a sampling of goods that 19th-century Californians coveted: china, wood saws and burlap sacks full of flour, rice and salt.

The Stars and Stripes were first raised in California on the Custom House flagpole. Monterey was named in 1602, founded in 1770 by Father Junipero Serra and was the Spanish capital of Alta California until the Mexicans revolted in 1822. Then Monterey was the Mexican capital until 1846, when Commodore John Drake Sloat landed here, raised the American flag and claimed California for the United States without firing a shot.

Follow the Path of History to California's first brick house and its delightful courtyard garden. A Virginian bought this land for $29, kilned his own bricks and built this simple home in 1847. Next door is the Whaling Station, headquarters of the Old Monterey Whaling Company from 1855 to 1885. At the time, whale blubber was sliced off and made into oil on the Custom House beach.

On the next corner is California's first theater. An enterprising sailor named Jack Swan built this wood and adobe structure in 1846 as a boarding house for sailors. In 1847, he produced his first play, with men in all the roles, and sold 100 tickets at $5 each. The theater was a success until 1849, when gold lured away his actors and the bulk of his audience.

Walk half a block to the Joseph Boston Store in the Casa del Oro. In 1849, Boston opened this store to serve the growing number of settlers brought in by the gold rush. Today, it reflects its late 19th-century beginnings, thanks to the Monterey History and Art Association.

Shelves are stocked with goods from that era: ribbons, tea, Victorian lace bags, rock candy, homemade bird houses and more. Proceeds from sales go to the Association. The safe in the corner once held prospectors' gold dust, as Boston's was the only safe in the region at the time. This is how a general mercantile store became a "Casa del Oro," or "House of Gold."

Walk down busy Pacific Street, past a series of quiet, simple adobes, to Colton Hall. A museum on the second floor recreates the room where California's first Constitutional Congress convened. Here they drafted the state's first Constitution and penned it in English and Spanish. Today, their top hats, quill pens and scattered papers remain as if the delegates had just taken a break.

These are a few of the more than 30 historic buildings on Monterey's Path of History. Other highlights include the Old Monterey Jail, with bleak granite walls from which no prisoner ever escaped, the Maritime Museum with exhibits on the area's nautical heritage, and the Larkin House, which focuses on home life in old Monterey.

Monterey's Path of History
Most buildings open daily 10-4.
Some open by guided tour only.
408/649-7118 (Monterey State Historic Park)
$2 Adults; $1 ages 6-17 for guided tours.
Package for all buildings is $4 Adults; $2 ages 6-17.

Benicia

Benicia was named for a beautiful, charming woman from a family steeped in history. Nearly 150 years later, you'll see that Benicia was aptly named. This state capital turned small town boasts several important historic sites, a number of handsomely renovated Victorians and a charming downtown with antique shops, cafes and boutiques.

Begin at the State Capitol building on the corner of 1st and G Streets. This imposing red brick structure fronted with two white, fluted columns was California's State Capitol for 13 months beginning in 1853. Since then it's been everything from a grammar school to the city jail.

Today, it's a State Historical Park. The Senate and Assembly rooms appear as though the early politicians are on a lunch break. Inkwells and candles wait on the desks, with spittoons on the floor nearby. Some men even left their top hats. (Open daily 10-5; $2 Adults, $1 ages 6-17, tel. 707/745-3385)

On weekend afternoons, you can tour the Fischer-Hanlon House next door. This circa-1858 home captures life in early California. It is fully furnished, complete with potbellied stoves, a creamery and an old-fashioned water pump in the pantry. The Fischer-Hanlon home is one of several charmingly restored Victorians along G Street.

The Brewery, a dark, cool saloon on H Street just north of the Capitol, is an unlikely spot for a history lesson. But its interior walls are covered with murals illustrating Benicia's grandest moments throughout the years. Browsers are welcome.

The colorful courtyard garden of St. Paul's Episcopal Church is two blocks north, at First and J Streets. This graceful edifice with Gothic details and colonial-style steeple was built in 1859 by shipwrights from Benicia's Pacific Mail and Steamship Company. The church's interior, with exposed, arched ceiling beams, resembles an upside-down ship's hull (open Sundays, Wednesdays and Holy Days).

St. Paul's rectory is a 1790 New England home which was dismantled, shipped around the Horn in 1868 and reassembled in Benicia. An attractive Queen Anne home, the Riddell-Fish House, is two blocks west of First Street on K Street.

Walk back down First Street towards the water. You may be enticed into the many antique shops and gift boutiques. Several cafes offer delicious, creative meals at reasonable prices. For something fancier, try the Union Hotel. This 1882 hotel is the oldest three-story structure in Benicia. Until 1952, its 20 rooms "came occupied," a subtle description for a bordello. Today it's been revamped as a bed and breakfast inn.

The renovated Tannery building, now filled with restaurants and boutiques, is a remnant of Benicia's tanning industry. This was once the principal tanning center of the Pacific Coast.

At a nearby spot on the waterfront, a spark began a wildfire that engulfed the entire nation. In May 1848, Sutter's messenger had stunning news: Gold discovered in the Sierra foothills. Before long, the thriving town of Benicia plunged to 14 families as men rushed to the Mother Lode.

Many of the buildings where First Street tapers into the water were bordellos. The abandoned green building was Jurgensen's Saloon in 1892. Jack London was among the regulars when he lived in a nearby houseboat. His stories "Tales of the Fish Patrol" and "John Barleycorn" are based partially on his experiences in Benicia.

The yellow building is the old transcontinental railroad depot. At the end of the pier, ferries carried thousands of passengers, including Pony Express riders, across the straits to and from Martinez. Today, park benches invite visitors to relax in quiet solitude overlooking the still waters.

Benicia Chamber of Commerce
601 1st St., Benicia 94510
707/745-2120

.◦ ◦• *Sonoma Plaza*

The toast of Sonoma wine country, this is one of the largest and prettiest plazas in California. You can spend an hour or an entire afternoon here, browsing in boutiques, exploring historic buildings or indulging in delicious homemade treats.

As you stroll around the plaza, take time to read the plaques which tell the history of the buildings. Many were built by the Vallejos in the 1830s and '40s when Sonoma was under Mexican rule.

Several businesses also boast long histories. A third-generation cheesemaker runs the Sonoma Cheese Factory. At the back of the store you can watch their specialty being created in 10,000-pound cheese vats. A slide show illustrates the history and process of cheesemaking.

The next corner is devoted entirely to history. The Sonoma State Historic Park encompasses this neighborhood of buildings, from the Servant's Quarters to the Mission. Venture into the barracks to discover the history of Sonoma. Exhibit rooms focus on the area's Indian, Mexican and American residents.

Seven nations have claimed Sonoma as their own: Spain, England, Russia, Mexican Empire, Mexican Republic, Bear Flag Republic and the United States. While under Mexican rule, Americans could not own land nor hold office.

In 1846, 30 Americans, self-proclaimed "Bears," revolted. They rode into town, surrounded Vallejo's home and, without firing a shot, seized the general and the town. They raised a crude muslin flag with a bear emblem, a symbol that would evolve into our state flag.

Built in 1823, the Mission San Francisco Solano de Sonoma is the northernmost and last of the California missions. It marks the end of 300 years of Spanish-Mexican settlement. Inside you will find up to 4-foot-thick adobe walls. In the chapel, the whitewashed walls are highlighted with borders of blue and gold designs. (Open daily 10-5, $2 Adults; $1 Children, tel. 707/938-1519)

The ancient-looking building across the street was once the Blue Wing Inn. Built about 1840, it boasts many renowned guests, including Ulysses S. Grant, Kit Carson and the bandit Murietta.

While walking up First Street, explore the vine-covered alleyways. Down El Paseo you will discover a delightful courtyard with an antique shop, millinery and pottery store, where you can buy handthrown pots and peek into the studio where they are created.

Drop by the Vasquez House, at the end of El Paseo, for friendly conversation and low-priced goodies baked by the Sonoma League for Historic Preservation volunteers. Built in 1856, the home was once owned by General Hooker, from whence the slang term originated for the ladies that catered to his soldiers.

Follow your nose to the Sonoma French Bakery, famous for their award-winning sourdough. Their secret? "Some people credit it to climate, but I think it's experience," said Josephine Morenzoni. She's been at the bakery for nearly 3 decades.

For more picnic goodies, try the Sonoma Sausage Co. across the plaza. They offer more than 30 deli meats and sausages, most of them homemade. Made-to-order sandwiches range from $3-$5.

Other stores around the plaza include thrift shops, a wine exchange, kitchen boutique and much more. If you're weary, relax in the old-fashioned saloon of the Sonoma Hotel.

Sonoma Plaza
Sonoma Valley Visitors Bureau
453 First St. (on the Plaza), Sonoma, CA 95476
707/996-1090

San Anselmo

When people visit the north Bay, they usually flock to Sausalito, Tiburon or the coast. But antique hounds will uncover a small paradise in San Anselmo, just a few miles west of the San Rafael Bridge.

Even if you're only a casual browser when it comes to antiques, you'll still find a slice of quintessential Marin County here. San Anselmo is small town America with a touch of open-minded eccentricity under an aura of affluence.

Antique shoppers don't have to go far to search out that special knick knack, brooch or curio cabinet. More than 130 dealers are clustered within a 1/2-mile. Sir Francis Drake Boulevard and San Anselmo Avenue, which runs one block to the west, are lined with antique shops, gift boutiques and cafes. Two-hour free parking is plentiful in the public lots and along the street. If you're planning to stay longer, park on the streets a few blocks west of town. It's not a far walk.

Pick up the free brochure, "Northern California's Antiques Capital," available at most San Anselmo antique stores. It lists the town's dealers, describes the kinds of items they carry and shows their locations on a map. You can follow along as you stroll through town or head directly for the kind of specialty antique store that interests you.

You may want to start your tour in The Pavilion, the distinctive building at the north end of town. Opened in 1980, their collective houses items from more than 30 dealers.

Amateur antiquers will appreciate The Pavilion's goal to label their goods with country of origin, date and, at times, the item's purpose. Here you'll find everything from cribs to crystal to quilts. For those who feel uncomfortable about bargaining, which is an accepted practice in many antique stores, The

Pavilion stands by its policy of "fair and firm" prices.

Nearby is the Modern i, which specializes in 1950s furniture and accessories. Oveda Maurer Antiques, on Greenfield, offers 18th-century and early 19th-century American furniture and accessories including pewter, early lighting, glass and folk art.

For English country furniture, especially pine, try the San Anselmo Country Store. Down the street, The Legacy, a collective of about 35 dealers, is the place to go for nostalgia and collectibles. One dealer specializes in antique radios.

Head one block west to San Anselmo Avenue, the heart of town. At the corner of Magnolia, peek into Fabled Lands, one of the more upscale shops. You may find unique pieces like an antique Indonesian baby carrier or Sumatran rice container.

Before leaving town, take a short drive up to San Anselmo's humble beginnings, the San Francisco Theological Seminary. To get there from San Anselmo Avenue, take a right on Bolinas at the south end of town, then take another right onto Kensington and follow the signs to Montgomery Hall.

You'll wind your way up a forested knoll to two surprising castle-like structures perched on the top of the hill. These are Montgomery and Scott Halls, built in 1892. The Seminary was the first real industry in San Anselmo. The 1906 earthquake convinced some people to settle down around it.

The completion of the Golden Gate Bridge in 1937 caused another influx in the population. In 1974, having grown to almost 13,000 residents, San Anselmo officially became a town. Today, the Seminary is a reminder of San Anselmo's quiet past while the town bustles below.

San Anselmo
Chamber of Commerce
P.O. Box 2844, San Anselmo 94979
415/454-2510

Sausalito

Sausalito combines the ambiance of a Mediterranean marina with a touch of Cape Cod clapboard and a history that's pure Marin. Just north of the Golden Gate Bridge, the town is an instant getaway.

Most visitors to this sunny tourist mecca spend their time on Bridgeway Boulevard. Here you'll find stores that offer everything from the wacky to the sublime, including designer toothbrushes, art deco sculpture, board games, resort-wear clothing, fine jewelry, handcrafts, t-shirts and souvenirs. Hawaiian ice cream, cookies and plenty of restaurants, many specializing in seafood, renew your energy.

When you've had enough shopping, explore Sausalito's quieter side. You can stroll along the shore or climb steep backstreets to visit pleasant parks, a poet's bench and a century-old church.

Sausalito has changed dramatically over the years, except for its knack for attracting those looking for the good life. In the late 1800s, the wealthy attempted to duplicate the life of the English country gentry in their Victorian mansions here.

In 1875, the railroad came to town, bringing transients and other unsavories along with it. Before long, the town boasted 25 gambling dens and bordellos, whose guests included the infamous Baby Face Nelson. During Prohibition, Sausalito bootleggers catered to San Francisco speakeasies.

In the 1950s and '60s, Sausalito was a magnet for artists seeking a bohemian lifestyle. The beat generation, flower power and funky houseboats were Sausalito trademarks.

Today, you can see remnants of all these phases of Sausalito's history. From Bridgeway, walk along the shore past restaurants cantilevered over the water. Horizons restaurant, built in 1898, was the first yacht club on the Pacific coast.

Bridgeway eventually ends at Valhalla, now The Chart House restaurant. It was opened in 1893 as a beer garden by a German native and used by bootleggers during Prohibition. Its best known owner was the colorful Sally Stanford, a former San Francisco madam and Sausalito mayor.

If you don't want to walk that far, look for the flower-bedecked Tiffany Park and climb the steep stairs to the back streets. At the top, turn right onto Tiffany. The Poet's Bench is at the next intersection. Carved into the stone bench is a poem about a castle of silence where "walls are draped with legends woven in threads of gold."

From here, follow Bulkley until you see the Alta Mira Hotel. Its sprawling patio topped with white, wrought iron furniture and light-colored umbrellas is especially popular with the Sunday brunch crowd. It is one of the three fancy hotels in Sausalito built in the late 1800s.

Across the street is the circa-1909 Presbyterian Church, with its cedar shingles and charming, uncluttered architecture. Follow the hill down from the church to the stairs leading back to Bridgeway. Below you is the colorful Vina Del Mar park with its fountain and elephant statues from the 1915 Panama-Pacific Exposition.

You'll come out by the 1885 Casa Madrona Hotel, which was a Beatnik beerhall-boarding house in the 1950s. Now it is a delightful bed and breakfast inn.

Next door is the Village Fair. Over the years, this was a Chinese gambling hall and opium den, then a distillery for bootleg whiskey, then an indoor golf course. Today it is an open air mall, complete with splashing waterfall. The Cafe Madrona on the third floor offers indoor and outdoor seating with superb views of the bay, a restful spot to enjoy an espresso and dessert.

Sausalito Chamber of Commerce
333 Caledonia Street, Box 566
Sausalito, CA 94966
415/332-0505

Mendocino

You may get a sense of déjà vu in Mendocino, even if you've never been here before. The town is Hollywood's favorite setting for shows set in charming New England towns, including "Murder, She Wrote," "The Russians are Coming," "Same Time Next Year" and "Dying Young."

We can thank Mendocino's first settlers for this slice of the east coast on the Pacific. They were loggers from New England, here to reap the bounty of the redwood forests. They built their down-east style Victorians along this rocky bluff abutting the ocean to reflect those homes left behind on another shore.

Today, tourism, not timber, is Mendocino's mainstay. The entire town is on the National Register of Historic Places. Almost all of the late 19th-century Victorian homes have been restored down to their fancy finials and fish-scale shingles. Many are unique bed and breakfast inns.

The ruggedly beautiful setting is a magnet for artists. The hub of the village boasts several galleries exhibiting their finely crafted exotic woods, watercolors depicting local scenery, contemporary jewelry and hand-thrown pottery.

To find the historical side of Mendocino, begin your tour at the Kelley House Museum. Housed in 1861 Victorian, the museum's historical photographs, artifacts and period furniture illustrate Mendocino's beginnings.

The house was built by State-of-Mainer William Henry Kelley, one of Mendocino's first pioneers. The promise of gold first lured him to California in 1850, but he soon discovered the untapped riches in the north coast's forests.

In the parlor, an impressive collection of historical photographs brings back the Mendocino of the late 1800s. A scene from 1865 shows lumber being sent down apron chutes from the top of the cliff at the end of town to the cargo ship in the waters below. Another from 1890 shows a 16-bull team pulling logs through the forest.

Society ladies began their long journey to San Francisco's shops by being lowered to the ship from the top of the headlands on a crude chair, which resembled a ski lift without the safety bar.

The Victorian era was not without its amenities, however, even in Mendocino. In the Kelley House guest room is a black horsehair loveseat and desk chair. Upstairs, the bedroom is highlighted with intricate stencilling along the top of the wall. This stencilling was meticulously reproduced from remnants of the original.

A walking tour around town reveals several architecturally intriguing structures scattered among the Victorians. The most distinctive building is the Presbyterian Church with its white, New England-style steeple. Built in 1867-'68, it is one of the oldest protestant churches in continuous use in California.

The small, bright red Kuan Ti Temple, on Albion between Kasten and Osborne, is the last remnant of the 200 Chinese who provided services for mill workers in the late 1800s.

Fans of "Murder, She Wrote" will recognize the Blair House, on the corner of Little Lake and Ford Streets. It serves as the exterior of Angela Lansbury's home in the popular television show. Interior scenes are shot in a Hollywood studio. It was built in 1888 for Elisha W. Blair who, like many of his neighbors, worked for the lumber mill.

All of these historic buildings add to Mendocino's welcome-to-the-past mystique, but it may best be found in what is not seen: no traffic lights, no parking meters and no mailboxes in this town where everybody seems to know their neighbor. Be forewarned, however, that many of Mendocino's residents were city folks who planned to visit for a few days, then moved here.

Mendocino
Fort Bragg/Mendocino Coast Chamber of Commerce
Box 1141, Fort Bragg, CA 95437
707/964-3153

Locke

The wooden buildings are ancient and weatherworn. Oriental characters are painted above the doors. In the Dai Loy gambling house, tables laid out with cards and dominos await the next player. Shops sell silk robes, embroidered linens and coolie hats.

No, this isn't a travelogue of exotic small town China. This is Locke, right here on the Sacramento River delta.

Locke is delta country's most unusual town. It was founded in 1912, the only rural town in the United States to be built entirely by Chinese. Today it is a ghost town that hasn't quite given up the ghost. Small shops sell inexpensive Chinese imports, antiques and giftware. There are two fine art galleries and a unique historic museum. To top it off, you can stop into Al's Place, a boisterous saloon and restaurant.

Begin your tour of Locke on the street below the levee road. On the eastern corner of this tiny town is a Chinese school. It is just one vestige of Locke's oriental heritage.

Tin San Chan founded this town on land owned by the three Locke brothers. Shortly after, he constructed its first building. The town boomed in 1915, when a fire destroyed nearby Walnut Grove and the displaced Chinese families moved to Locke. In addition to the school, Locke once boasted a church, theater, two saloons, five grocery stores, six restaurants and five hotels and rooming houses. The riverboat and train made regular stops here.

Today, Locke's Main Street is a photographers' paradise of weatherworn, western front buildings. Some are so rickety that they're buckling to the side, as if a good gust of wind will blow them over.

The most intriguing spot in town is the Dai Loy Museum. This is, literally, a time capsule of a gambling house that operated here from 1916 to

1950. When the gambling house closed down, they simply locked the doors, leaving it all behind. When the doors were opened years later, everything in the room was still intact.

Inside, gaming cards, dominos and dice games wait on the tables. Displays explain the rules of each unusual game. Fan-Tan was played with ordinary white buttons.

The gamblers were heavy smokers. Strips of sandpaper were attached to the edge of the tables for lighting matches. The tables' cross braces are well worn by the years of nervous feet.

This unusual collection includes the butterfly harp that originally was played here. Any patron who wanted to grace the gambling hall with music could borrow it.

The Lottery Room, its twirling wire basket full of ping pong balls marked with Chinese characters, is not too unlike today's lotteries. Another exhibit room illustrates the importance of the Chinese laborers who built the levees and islands of the delta. Artifacts also include China bowls, small medicine bottles and an English and Chinese newspaper from the late 1930s that had been used as padding beneath a table top.

Near the Dai Loy is the River Road Gallery, which specializes in fine art paintings and pottery. Next door, Locke Ness is a small but fun antiques store.

Lotus Gifts specializes in toys and embroidered silk clothing. At Peony Imports, you can buy crocheted placemats, patchwork guest towels or a coolie hat for a few dollars, all made in China. Climb the alley's wooden steps up to the main levee road to Locke China Imports for the most varied selection of Chinese goods. And if visiting the laid-back delta country hasn't relieved all your stress, a Chinese Acupressure practice on Main Street offers a 15-minute treatment for $20.

Dai Loy Museum
Locke, Sacramento River Delta
Fri. 11-4:30; Sat. & Sun. 11-5
$1 Adults; $.50 Student; $.25 Children under 12

.. ••*Old Sacramento*

Where else can you can determine your weight in gold, communicate to a friend via telegraph and guess the functions of odd-shaped iron hardware tools? Nowhere but Old Sacramento. Within two blocks are five fun history museums that focus on the capital's formative years.

The Central Pacific Railroad Depot is a reconstruction of where you would have arrived back in 1876. The new transcontinental railroad shortened the cross-country transit time from at least 3 months by ship or wagon to a breakneck 2 weeks. The depot bustled with travelers, freight wagons and hawkers. Shipments arrived by boat from San Francisco and were loaded onto trains for destinations in and beyond the Sierra.

Today, the station is restored to its 1870s heyday. An audio wand brings back the sounds of the era. Voices of passengers, a baggage man and others tell lively stories you might have overheard then. Locomotives wait on the tracks in this cavernous, shed-like building as if frozen in time.

Across the street is the Sacramento History Center. It's housed in a reconstruction of the 1854 City Hall and Waterworks building which originally occupied this site. Inside, you're taken on a chronological tour of local history. You pass a replica of an Indian hut made of tule leaves and willow, a miner's shack, a Japanese internment cabin and more. The agricultural exhibit room includes a recreated 1928 kitchen set up for canning fruit. Above your head, cans tumble along the working prototype of the Blue Diamond almond canning line.

One highlight is the museum's $1 million collection of Mother Lode gold. Nearby, stand on the large scale and find your weight in gold both by 1849 standards, when it sold for $20 per troy ounce, and in 1987, when it sold for $450 per troy ounce.

Then try your luck at panning. Gold pans, covered with clear plastic, contain dirt with just enough water for swirling. Follow the instructions and, before long, real gold specks appear through the black mud.

Next door is the often-overlooked Huntington & Hopkins Hardware Store. This is a time capsule of the late 1800s. You can guess the function of the odd-shaped tools of the era and purchase baskets, iron nails, wash basins and other items that the store's original customers bought.

The B.F. Hastings building at 2nd and J Streets held the offices of the Alta Telegraph Company in 1859. Today, artifacts in the museum include a working telegraph. Sit in one booth and communicate to a friend in the booth across the room. Posters in each booth display the Morse Code.

This building also was the terminus for the Pony Express and has housed the Wells Fargo bank since 1854. Among the collection of antique handwritten receipts and a scale for weighing gold is the new juxtaposed against the old--a computerized automatic teller machine.

Central Pacific Railroad Depot
Front & K Sts., tel. 916/445-4209
Open daily 10-5
$5 Adults; $2 ages 6-17; includes admission
to California State Railroad Museum.

Sacramento History Center
101 I St., tel. 916/449-2057
Tu.-Sun. 10-4:30
$3 Adults; $1.50 ages 6-17.

Huntington & Hopkins Hardware Store
115 I St., tel. 916/445-4209
Tu.-Sun. 10-5
Free

B.F. Hastings Building and Wells Fargo
2nd and J Sts., tel. 916/445-4209
Tu.-Sun. 10-5
Free

---

*Extra Tip...*See page 91 to find out how you can save money on admission to Sacramento's historic museums.

Truckee

In the 1870s, it had the second largest Chinatown on the Pacific coast, a testament to the manpower behind the transcontinental railroad's route through the Sierra. Today the railroad still stops in Truckee and the town clings to its old west flair.

Truckee is a favorite stop for people zooming along Interstate 80 or heading down to Tahoe. Many pause to stretch their legs, grab a bite to eat or peek into the boutique windows. But Truckee is fast becoming a destination in its own right.

Truckee is a working man's town on the verge of gentrification. A freight train clatters along one side of the street. A boutique plays the soft, contemporary music of George Winston on the other. An upscale gallery spotlights the newest art trend next to a general store selling go-fish games.

The best place to start your tour of Truckee is in the train station. Here you will find dozens of brochures and information sheets on the town and the surrounding area. You can pick up everything from the North Tahoe/Truckee tabloid with its discount coupons on nearby attractions and restaurants to a Walking Tour of Historic Truckee.

Truckee's history dates back to 1844 when a Native American chief whose name sounded like "Tro-kay" became a favorite guide for westward pioneers. Before long, the river and nearby lake were called Truckee. The lake is now called Donner after the ill-fated pioneer family who was snowbound near here in the winter of 1846. Many starved. The survivors lived by resorting to cannibalism.

In 1863, the first log cabin was built in what is now the center of town. The building still remains, though at the turn of the century it was rolled on logs to its present site on Church Street.

Truckee boomed in 1868 with the building of the transcontinental railroad. The Chinese worked on its construction but were ostracized and forced to move across the river in 1879. Less than a decade later, the whites drove away all the Chinese. Just across the river is the last remnant of their population. The white building that is now a sign shop was built in 1878 as a Chinese herb shop.

The avenue behind Commercial Row, now called Jibboom Street, was once Truckee's red light district. Today you can see the jail that was used from 1875 to 1964. It's rumored that Baby Face Nelson once spent the night here.

Shoppers enjoy the variety along Truckee's Commercial Row. One of the best places to buy athletic clothes is the Sports Outlet on the western end of town. Skiers, cyclists, hikers and joggers will find good quality outfits at discount prices.

In the next building, you can watch as artists create bronze ships and delicate glass flowers. With a flaming torch, James Hacker welds and molds metals into a deer, a skier or a hawk. Frank Rossbach uses a torch to form glass into graceful, slender wine glasses, hummingbirds or calla lilies.

A delightful break from the upscale boutiques and galleries, the Truckee Variety Co. is a favorite hang-out for local kids. This is an old-fashioned five & dime, with counters full of novelty toys, jars brimming with candy and basics like plastic foam hair rollers and glue sticks.

Don't miss the Earthsongs cellar shop if you're a tea-lover. Shelves of jars feature more than 40 different teas, from Vanilla to Mad Hatter to Treasure Island Mint. More jars contain exotic spices.

The ArtTruckee gallery features first-class works from area artists, including limited edition prints of local scenery, so you can bring a piece of Truckee home with you.

Truckee-Donner Chamber of Commerce
and Visitors Bureau
10065 Commercial Row, Box 2757
Truckee, CA 96160
800/548-8388 or 916/587-2757

Volcano

Located 12 curvy miles off State Route 49, the beaten path in these parts, this is the gold country town that tourism forgot. Pick-up trucks have replaced freight wagons and mountain bikes stand at hitching posts, but not much else has changed in Volcano since the 49ers' boom fizzled out.

Today, it recaptures the quiet post-gold-rush era, with a few fun gift stores and a couple of small restaurants along a cobblestone walk. Benches invite you to set a spell and soak up history.

As early as 1848, veterans of the Mexican War discovered gold here. They named their settlement Soldier's Gulch, a more accurate name than the later Volcano, inspired by the mistaken idea that the town lay in a volcanic crater.

By 1851, Volcano erupted into a boomtown. Miners soon averaged $100 per day per man. During the 1850s, buildings sprang up: the Adams Express Building, Sieble's Brewery, the Jail, the I.O.O.F. and Masonic Hall and the Union Hotel Billiards, Saloon and Boarding House.

Surprisingly, secluded Volcano became rich in culture as well. California's first rental library, the Miner's Library Association, was established here in 1850. Four years later, the Volcano Thespian Society initiated the state's first little theater group. Volcano also boasted California's first literary and debating society, first private law school and first observatory, built just two miles away.

Suddenly, in the late 1850s, the placer miners began coming up empty. A frenetic foray into hydraulic mining tore at the surrounding hillsides, sending rivers of mud into the village below, nearly destroying the town.

As late as 1862, an optimistic entrepreneur built a three-story hotel, the St. George, at one end of town. At the time it was the tallest and one of the most elegant hotels in the Mother Lode. But by

1865, the rest of the gold played out. Fortune-seekers rushed to more promising veins, leaving Volcano behind.

As the dust settled, vacant stone buildings became the only reminders of the once-thriving village. Volcano was tucked neatly under a bell jar, preserved in time and spirit for generations to come.

Today, the St. George Hotel is still the largest and, for Volcano, the most elegant building in town. It rents out rooms decorated much the way that hopeful prospectors would have seen them.

Along one side of Volcano's short stretch of Main Street, stone ruins form the backdrop for Volcano's outdoor theater and small park. On the other side, weather-worn stone buildings house the town's few businesses. The Country Store is the local gathering place. Its warped shelves are packed with cans of stew, hunting supplies and other goods that could have been stocked 100 years ago. In the back of the store, a skylight brightens a small lunch room with an old oven built into the stone wall.

Down the cobblestone sidewalk, shaded by a slumping wood overhang, is the Jug and Rose Confectionery. Inside, you'll find an old-fashioned soda fountain and a small cafe.

The small shed next to the mineral shop houses one of the two landmarks that symbolize Volcano's community pride and quirky personality. "Old Abe," a bronze cannon, was acquired by Unionist miners during the Civil War to protect their gold from Confederate sympathizers. Their ammunition? Stones from the creek bed.

Across the street, you'll find the historical landmark sign for Volcano, originally placed four miles away. In 1934, a proposed dam would have flooded Volcano, but the plan was negated by geology and water rights. In 1980, the residents placed their own plaque here proclaiming that historic Volcano didn't drown, "not by a dam site!"

Volcano
Amador County Chamber of Commerce
2048 West Highway 88, Martell, CA 95654
800/649-4988 or 209/223-0350

Notes

Literary Landmarks

Robinson Jeffers' Tor House

Robinson Jeffers is considered by many Californians to be one of our state's greatest poets. But even if you aren't a Jeffers' fan, you'll enjoy touring his Tor House in Carmel.

Jeffers' rustic home and stone Hawk Tower are an oasis of old Carmel, when the natural beauty of the Pacific's rugged coast attracted artists, poets and writers rather than expensive shopping malls and exclusive resorts.

Jeffers chose the site and began construction on the Tor House in 1918, naming it for the craggy knoll, or "tor," on which it stood. He wrote all his major works and most of his poetry here and eventually died in this humble home in 1962.

With the Pacific for a backdrop, distinctive and romantic Hawk Tower is a scene out of ancient Ireland. Jeffers built the tower by himself, learning the art of making "stone love stone" by apprenticing with the contractor building his house. Begun in 1920, the tower took four years to complete. It became a treasured retreat for his beloved wife, Una, and a magical playground for their twin sons.

The tower walls are six feet thick at its base, enclosing two small rooms. One has Jeffers' sturdy chair, constructed from the burnt timbers of the nearby Carmel Mission. A narrow, spiraling secret passage climbs up the tower to Una's room.

Despite the rough stone exterior, this room is cozy with warm wood paneling and gothic-arched windows. In one corner is Una's small organ. Pictures of towers in Ireland echo the theme of Hawk Tower.

An epigram carved in the wooden mantle of the fireplace reads, "they make their dreams for themselves," truly reflecting the Jeffers' lifestyle.

Jeffers incorporated artifacts from around the world in his building. The porthole in the stairway is from Napoleon's ship. The red stone at the very top of the tower is from the Great Wall of China.

His Tor house also is reminiscent of old Europe. It is modeled after a Tudor barn in England. The simple home is furnished as when Jeffers lived here. The Steinway is the same piano Gershwin played when he visited.

Books, many poetry or Thomas Hardy, crowd the shelves. Records show Jeffers had read almost all of his 3,500 volumes.

Pictures and statues of unicorns are placed throughout the home. The immense, spear-like horn of a narwhale, the closest thing to a unicorn horn that Una could find, hangs in the dining hall. This medieval room is furnished with a rough wooden table and benches.

Highlighting the stone walls are more intriguing artifacts, small Mayan and Inca masks. At the very peak of the A-frame wall is a stone from the great pyramid at Giza.

Throughout the tour, Jeffers poetry is read. "The Bed by the Window," a 1932 poem, was written about the bed where Jeffers died in the Tor House. The window in this bedroom is built low in the wall so a person could lie on the bed and just turn his head to see the rocky shore of Jeffers' cherished Point Lobos.

Originally, a small, understated sign reading, "not at home," hung on Jeffers' door to steer away unwanted guests, but friends knew enough to ignore it. Now, through the Robinson Jeffers Tor House Foundation, you, too, are invited into the poet's private sanctuary and a unique look at old Carmel.

Robinson Jeffers' Tor House
Ocean View Ave., Carmel
408/624-1813 or 408/624-1840 when home is open
Open by guided tour only; reservations advised.
Tours on the hour, Fri. & Sat. 10-3.
$5 Adults; $3.50 College students;
$1.50 High School students
No children under 12 admitted.

Eugene O'Neill's Tao House

The Chinese characters riveted to the black courtyard gate of Eugene O'Neill's Tao House proclaim it is the "House of the Righteous Way." Cradled in the rolling hills of Danville, the troubled playwright believed he had found his beloved last home and harbor here.

During the Tao House years, from 1937 to 1944, O'Neill penned such classics as "The Iceman Cometh," "Hughie," "Moon for the Misbegotten" and "A Long Day's Journey Into Night." He was honored with four Pulitzer Prizes and is the only American playwright to be awarded the Nobel Prize for Literature.

Both Eugene and his wife, Carlotta, were attracted to the precepts of Taoism and carried them through the design of their home. The brick courtyard walk makes four turns before reaching the front door, since Taoists believe that evil spirits only travel in straight lines.

The original green-hued mirror and a series of masks in the entranceway are the first indication of the house's brooding, introverted atmosphere. Oriental "Fu" dogs, believed to protect against evil spirits, guard the staircase.

Like the Fu dogs, Carlotta was fiercely protective of O'Neill. She routinely held back visitors and correspondence from O'Neill if she deemed it would interfere with his writing.

An oriental rug and ceramic elephant match those in the period photograph of the livingroom, once filled with Oriental-style furniture from Gump's.

Oona, O'Neill's daughter from his second marriage, was one of the few visitors to stay in the guest room. O'Neill virtually disowned Oona over her marriage to Charlie Chaplin, a thrice-divorced man O'Neill's age, who was involved in a scandalous paternity suit. O'Neill's first-born son, Eugene Jr., committed suicide. His only other child, Shane, was a drug addict. O'Neill once called him "a complete rotter." Shane also killed himself, though long after his father's death.

O'Neill and Carlotta enjoyed some of their happiest times in Rosie's room. Rosie was O'Neill's favorite entertainment, a player piano from a bordello. Their Dalmatian, Blemie, as cherished and pampered as any child, slept here.

Today, an exact model of Rosie stands along one wall, the original blue phonograph cupboard along another. Photographs of O'Neill's father, mother and friends fill the room.

O'Neill's study hides in a secluded corner on the second floor. With wood paneling and beams, it resembles a ship's cabin. A collection of sailing ship models are prominently displayed.

O'Neill's original blue velvet chair sits at the desk. A blank pad of paper seems to be waiting for the playwright to return. Even a crumbled pack of Lucky Strikes, found by the Park Service in the recesses of the fireplace, evokes O'Neill's presence.

But even as O'Neill was creating his greatest works, a serious tremor rapidly diminished his physical ability to write. O'Neill's entire manuscript for "The Emperor Jones" is little over five pages of virtually unreadable handwriting.

O'Neill's failing health and the lack of household help and transportation during wartime forced them to sell their home. O'Neill once told Carlotta if he could not write, he would die. They knew they were facing more than the end of their time at Tao House. Before they left, they burned several of O'Neill's unfinished works in the fireplace. O'Neill died in a Boston hotel room nine years later.

Eugene O'Neill National Historic Site
Tours meet at the Danville public parking lot
on Railroad Ave.
510/838-0249
Tours Wed.-Sun. 10 & 12:30; maximum 11 per tour
By advance reservation only
Free

Heinhold's First and Last Chance Saloon

Listen carefully at Heinhold's First and Last Chance Saloon on the Oakland waterfront. You may hear the kind of high seas tales that inspired Jack London's books. For more than a century, sailors have haunted Heinhold's. Today's Navy now sits on stools worn by yesterday's oyster pirates.

Even if you've never set foot on a ship, you'll enjoy this fun step into history. The first dizzying experience is the floor that slants downward, a balancing test even for those with sea legs. The slant was caused when the pilings beneath sank into the mud during the 1906 earthquake.

The trembler also stopped the clock in the saloon. Like the floor, the clock has never been fixed. It's now part of Heinhold's unique personality.

Once something finds its way into Heinhold's, it's there to stay. Every inch of wall, ceiling and rafter is covered with an eclectic array of mementos in this cozy museum-cum-bar.

Built in 1880 with the timbers of an old whaling ship, the funky cabin was first used as a bunkhouse for men working nearby oyster beds. It became Heinhold's Saloon in 1883.

Today, you'll be sitting at the same rough, wooden tables where Jack London, President William Howard Taft and Robert Louis Stevenson have imbibed over the years. The dim lights above are the original gas fixtures, making Heinhold's the only commercial operation in California that still uses them.

The stove is original and was Heinhold's only source of heat until 1989. Also squeezed into this tiny saloon are the original movie machine and the timeworn bar and rail.

One wall is dedicated to photographs of Jack London. As a young boy, London studied his school books on the docks until Heinhold invited him in out of the rain. London's favorite spot was the round corner table, as evidenced by the photo of him sitting there studying.

London met the salty characters who peopled his books right here in Heinhold's. Alexander McLean, known for his cruelty on his so-called "Hell Ship," became Wolf Larsen in The Sea Wolf. Heinhold and his saloon are mentioned 17 times in John Barleycorn and The Tales of the Fish Patrol.

Heinhold also loaned London the money to attend college and helped London in his deals for his three ships, the Razzle Dazzle, the Snark and the Roamer. All three deals were struck in this saloon.

Through the years, customers have added their own mementos to Heinhold's collection. Money from around the world is signed and tacked to the wall so that sailors leaving port will have payment for a drink on their return. The plaques dedicated to Heinhold's saloon are from four aircraft carriers.

Most pervasive are business cards tacked one on top of the other on every free speck of wall. Many are blackened with decades of smoke from the stove, lanterns, cigarettes and creosote in the old wood.

On a sunny afternoon or balmy evening, pull yourself away from Heinhold's for a stroll around the waterfront. Next to the saloon is the 1897 log cabin where Jack London lived while prospecting the Klondike gold rush. It was authenticated and moved here piece by piece.

Nearby, Jack London Village is a two-level wooden pier area with a fun selection of specialty shops and restaurants. Many have a superb view of the water and marina with the San Francisco skyline on the horizon.

Heinhold's First and Last Chance Saloon
Jack London Square, Oakland waterfront
510/839-6761
Mon.-Th. Noon-11 p.m.;
Fri. & Sat. Noon-1 A.M.; Sun. Noon-8 P.M.
Free

John Muir Historic Site

"I care to live only to entice people to look at nature's loveliness," John Muir wrote to a friend. You, too, can share in nature's loveliness when you visit Muir's house and the small but thriving parcel of his original fruit ranch in Martinez.

Muir's tireless writing from his "scribble den" in this stately Victorian popularized a radical concept—conservation—at a crucial time when land exploitation was quickly depleting vast areas of forest. Proving that the pen was mightier than the wood saw, his letters and subsequent meeting in Yosemite with Teddy Roosevelt convinced the President to establish 148 million acres of National Forest, 5 national Parks and 23 National Monuments during his term in office.

Muir co-founded and was first president of the Sierra Club and was key in establishing the National Park Ranger Service. We enjoy Yosemite, Sequoia, Mount Rainier, Arizona's Petrified Forest and Grand Canyon National Parks today thanks to Muir's turn-of-the-century battles.

Appropriately, Muir's property is now part of the National Park Service. The imposing gray Victorian, its entrance flanked by towering century-old palms, was built by Muir's father-in-law, John Strentzel, in 1882. Ironically, although Muir lived here the last 24 years of his life, it does not reflect the mountain man's simple tastes. It's built almost entirely of redwood, the tree Muir devoted his life to protecting.

The home has been lovingly restored to the time when Muir lived here. Restorers relied on the memories of people who visited with Muir as their guide. A custom-made black horsehair sofa once again adorns the west parlor. The replacement marble in the fireplace came from the original quarry in Italy. Even the floor is finished in a technique thought forgotten.

The 1906 earthquake gave Muir a chance to show his architectural style. After the chimney of the coal-burning marble fireplace in the east parlor was destroyed, he replaced it with an immense, brick, mission-style wood burner. Finally, Muir was able to enjoy a "real mountain campfire" in his home.

But Muir spent his most precious time in the dining room. He treasured the moments with his family and employed a clever strategy to ensure his two daughters came to dinner on time. He told a continuing story at each meal, leaving off at a cliffhanger. One of these stories eventually was published as Stickeen, the endearing tale of his heroic canine companion in Alaska.

The most important room in the house is Muir's study, which he called his "scribble den." Muir's research papers, articles, book manuscripts and letters lay strewn about the floor as though he were still in the midst of a fight for conservation.

Symbols of two of Muir's proudest triumphs are displayed next to the desk—the yellow hood of his honorary doctorate from Yale and a spear presented to him by native Alaskans for his courage in exploring the living glaciers. A bowl of dried bread balls, Muir's favorite snack, waits on the mantel.

Beyond the orchard is the 1849 Martinez Adobe, built by Don Vicente on what once was his 17,000-acre Mexican land grant. Muir's daughter, Wanda, called the adobe home during the last years of his life. Muir would visit daily to dine and play with his grandchildren.

Here you can picnic among the fruit trees and reflect on Muir's belief that "the clearest way into the universe is through a forest wilderness."

John Muir National Historic Site
Alhambra Ave., just off Rte. 4, Martinez
510/228-8860
Wed.-Sun. 10-4:30
$1 Adults 17-61; Seniors and Children Free

Jack London State Historic Park

Jack London was, and still is, one of the most popular authors in the world. To many, he epitomizes the robust, adventuresome, free-thinking American. Nowhere is his style more evident than at the 800-acre Jack London State Historic Park in Glen Ellen.

Here, you can see the haunting ruins of Wolf House, London's dream castle. Nearby, the stone House of Happy Walls serves as monument and museum to the author. It houses such eclectic memorabilia as dancing sticks from the Solomons, London's photographs of the Japanese-Russian War and the first of his 600 rejection letters.

The sprawling grounds also encompass London's small cottage, where he lived and worked while Wolf House was being built, a horse barn, the remains of his pig palace and a delightful picnic area.

Begin your tour at the House of Happy Walls. London's wife, Charmian, began construction of this house three years after London's death as a memorial to her late husband. Charmian was the first curator, so everything is authentic. London's books, letters, a scale model of his ship, the Snark, exotic souvenirs and other displays tell the story of London's adventurous life.

London's study has been relocated here from their modest cottage, now under restoration, where he wrote all his later works and, ultimately, died. The roll-top desk, with paper and ink at the ready, appears as though London had just left after completing his 1,000-word-a-day ritual.

Follow the half-mile forested trail to Wolf House. Visitors are dwarfed by the ghostly castle walls and granite chimneys that compete with the redwoods for a piece of the sky. London sunk the bulk of his earnings from writing into this immense castle. He harvested monolithic stones from the surrounding Valley of the Moon and fortified them with mighty redwood timber, sure that it would shelter generations of his heirs. Tragically, a fire of suspicious origin burned Wolf House to the ground days before London and his wife, Charmian, were due to take residence in 1913.

Today, the timbers are long gone and weeds blossom in the hearths. But you can imagine London's dream castle by studying the floor plans displayed by the ruins. A two-story living room, a dining room that could seat 50 and numerous guest rooms reveal London's gregarious nature. Wolf House was to have a gun and trophy room, a sleeping tower, even a stag party room.

London also glowed over his "Pig Palace," located near the cottage. He designed the innovative piggery with the hope that it would revolutionize pig farming. Instead, his stock died of pneumonia, but the ruins of the piggery and nearby silo, the first and biggest concrete silo in the state, stand as testimony to London's audacious spirit.

If you're a Jack London fan, don't miss the World of Jack London bookstore, about a mile south of the park on Arnold Drive in Glen Ellen. Owner Russ Kingman is an internationally recognized London biographer.

He's also an avid collector of London memorabilia. Over the years he's acquired and sold nearly $300,000 of it. He owns all of London's first editions, some very rare proof copies, copies of Charmian's diaries, even a lock of London's hair snatched at the crematorium. Kingman is determined to discover what London did every day of his existence and has 75,000 index cards to prove it. So if you have any questions about Jack London, ask Kingman.

Jack London State Historic Park
2400 London Ranch Rd., Glen Ellen
707/938-5216
Park open daily 8-5; museum open daily 10-5
Closed Jan. 1, Thanksgiving and Christmas
$5 per car; $4 if senior is in car

Mark Twain in Gold Country

The gold rush was one of the wildest times in the west and no one had more fun chronicling it than Mark Twain. His yen for travel and wry sense of humor were an open book for the tall tales of eccentric miners.

Angels Camp and Murphy's proved to be gold mines for the writer's pen. Both towns still retain the flavor of the old west. Today, you can visit the 1855 Angels Hotel, where Twain heard the story, "The Celebrated Jumping Frog of Calaverous County," that brought him and Angels Camp to immortal fame. On a secluded hillside nearby, you can peek into the windows of a replica of the crude wooden cabin where Twain actually penned the tale.

Samuel Clemens (Twain's real name) first came west in 1861. After trying his hand at mining, he became a reporter for the <u>Virginia City Enterprise</u> in Nevada. Here, he chose his pen name, Mark Twain, after a common riverboat pilot's call in his native state of Missouri. In 1864, Twain came to Angels Camp, already a bustling gold rush town.

The area boomed early in the rush. By 1849, some 4,500 miners were prospecting here. Angel was the name of a merchant who grew wealthy by digging into the pockets of the miners, rather than digging for gold in the mines. Clothing and tools sold for astronomical prices.

Before long, the placer gold played out and the boom might have busted but for a man named Bennager Raspberry. Raspberry was hunting when his ramrod got stuck in his gun. Since he couldn't knock it out, he pointed his gun towards the ground and shot it out. The ramrod pierced the ground and revealed the unmistakable shine of gold-bearing quartz. Within three days, Raspberry mined $10,000 worth.

Raspberry's story may be just another tall tale, but it wouldn't be the only one to come out of Angel's Camp. While sitting in the Angels Hotel, a two-story brick building with iron shutters on Main Street on the south end of town, Twain was told the story of the "Celebrated Jumping Frog."

It seems that a compulsive better, Jim Smiley, caught a frog. He "cal'klated to edercate him" and "learn that frog to jump." A stranger came to town and challenged him to a jumping contest between his animal and an ordinary, "unedercated" frog. The stranger then deviously poured a load of buckshot down the throat of Smiley's frog. Sure enough, the frog couldn't budge and Smiley lost his bet.

When printed back east, this simple story propelled Angels Camp and Mark Twain to fame. Today, the frog motif can still be found in several of the gift stores and tourist sites in town. Angels Camp even holds an annual jumping frog contest, usually the third weekend in May.

To reach the replica of the author's cabin, head south on State Route 49 and look closely for the sign to Mark Twain's cabin on the east side of the street. A steep, curvy road brings you to the cabin.

This is Jackass Hill. It once served as an overnight grazing spot for the hundreds of pack animals that transported miner's supplies from boomtown to boomtown.

A quick detour off Highway 4 east of State Route 49 leads to Murphy's, one of gold country's best preserved relics. Twain stayed at Murphy's Hotel, once considered one of the finest hotels on the Mother Lode. Today, you can still visit Murphy's hotel or stroll along Main Street, which appears to have stood still in time, and imagine it as Twain saw it. While others around him mined for gold, Twain found his fortune in stories of the Mother Lode.

Calaverous County Visitor Center
1301 S. Main St., P.O. Box 637
Angels Camp, CA 95222
209/736-0049 or 800/999-9039
Free

Notes

❦ *Japanese Tea Garden* & *The Conservatory*

There are two unique stems in Golden Gate Park's bouquet of gardens that blossom with history as well as beauty. They are the Japanese Tea Garden and The Conservatory.

The Japanese Tea Garden, created in 1894 for the California International Exposition, is the oldest tea garden in the United States. It now encompasses five acres of gracefully landscaped ornamental trees, ponds teeming with carp, temple gates, arched bridges, a five-tiered Shinto pagoda, a bonsai forest and two-century-old Buddha.

A stroll through the gardens was aptly described as "stepping into a picture" by the respected *Horticulture* magazine. Each turn brings you closer to the beauty of nature and your place in it.

Japanese maples, Oriental magnolias, camellias, azaleas, dwarf cypresses, cedars and pines blend in perfect harmony. Although this is one of the most popular spots in Golden Gate Park, a sense of solitude and tranquility pervades.

Amidst this oasis of serenity, the open air Tea House serves tea and cookies. Now a standard in any oriental restaurant, fortune cookies were invented here by the garden's creator, Makoto Hagiwara, in 1914 to amuse his guests.

The Conservatory is one of Golden Gate Park's crown jewels. This graceful crystal palace is the park's oldest structure and is the oldest growing house in California. It is listed on the National Register of Historic Sites.

The Conservatory's Victorian-era accents and central dome are designed after the greenhouse in London's Kew Gardens. It was built in England, and its 33 tons of glass were shipped around Cape Horn to San Francisco in 1875 at the bequest of millionaire James Lick. But Lick died the following year and the crates remained unopened on his estate in San Jose.

Public-minded citizens made the Conservatory a reality for all to enjoy. The greenhouse was purchased and erected in the park in 1879. Tragically, their efforts were dashed by a fire in 1883 which virtually destroyed the dome. Railroad baron Charles Crocker came to the rescue, donating $10,000 for its restoration. It miraculously survived the 1906 earthquake and greets visitors now as it has for more than a century.

Crossing the hothouse threshold is like stepping into the tropics. The most striking specimen is the towering plant that fills the central dome. With its three-foot-long leaves, it appears to be a rare rain-forest giant. In fact, it is a 110-year-old philodendron, one of the most common houseplants.

Strolling through this indoor garden, you'll discover delicate orchids, sweetly scented hibiscus and special seasonal exhibits. An old-fashioned gazebo invites visitors to rest a spell, surrounded by the flourishing green, and enjoy this beautiful legacy of our Victorian past.

Japanese Tea Garden
Next to the Asian Art Museum, Golden Gate Park
415/752-1171
Open daily 9-6:30.
Tea House open daily 10:30-5:30
$2 Adults; $1 Seniors 65 and over and ages 6-12
First and last half-hour free;
Free first Wed. of each month
($1.30 for tea and cookies)
The Conservatory
Kennedy Drive, Golden Gate Park
415/666-7017
Open daily 9-5 (until 6 during Daylight Savings Time)
$1.50 Adults;
$.75 Seniors 65 and over and ages 6-12
First and last half-hour free;
Free first Wed. of each month and major holidays

🌸 *Hakone Gardens*

Deep in the woods of Saratoga, just south of San Jose, a surprising slice of old Japan invites you to enjoy peaceful harmony with nature. This is Hakone Japanese Gardens, a 75-year-old canvas of sculpted trees, splashing waterfalls and still reflecting ponds, punctuated with traditional Japanese houses.

This land was part of the 16-acre summer estate of Oliver and Isabel Stine of San Francisco. In 1917, Mrs. Stine spent six months in Japan to follow her artistic bent. She was captivated with Japanese gardens and the Fuji-Hakone National Park.

Upon her return to California, Stine hired an Imperial gardener to create her Hakone Gardens. It is patterned after a traditional 17th-century Zen garden. A Japanese architect designed her home and the Upper House to harmonize with the landscape.

The main gate, or Mon, was added in 1932 by Major Charles Lee Tilden, who owned the gardens at that time. The City of Saratoga purchased it in 1966 for all to enjoy, hiring a Japanese specialist to ensure the garden's continued authenticity.

A sense of timelessness prevails in Hakone. Visitors in the early 1900s were as equally entranced as today's tourists. The Mon is still a magic threshold from modern world to ancient orient.

A medley of splashing water draws you to the hill and pond garden. A wooden bridge arches over one side of the reflecting pond. Below, bright gold and white carp, or koi, swim gracefully through the water. The shaded wooden Wisteria Pavilion on the opposite bank is an inviting respite on a sunny day.

Your gaze is drawn up the hillside to the Upper House, with its simple lines and pagoda-style roof. This is the Moon Viewing House, designed by a Japanese master craftsman in 1917. It was built in the traditional samurai style, without nails. Its exterior was treated to lend the proper look of age.

You're welcome to stroll onto the veranda, or engawa, which wraps around three sides of the house. It offers one of the finest views of the hill and pond garden below. Peer through the windows to see the traditional tatami mats placed neatly on the floor of this one open, uncluttered room.

A Wisteria-entwined arborway leads to the Upper Pavilion, another inviting spot to contemplate the gardens. Paths wind across the hillside to one of Hakone's newest additions, the Kizuna-En, or Bamboo Garden.

Not long ago, this 2-acre garden was a tangled jungle of brush and trees. Now it is a sea of delicate greens, with the swirl of a white pebble pathway and precisely placed stones. This is a joint effort between Saratoga and their Japanese sister city, Muko-shi. It symbolizes their international partnership. The white gravel area represents the Pacific ocean, with 5 large stones as the local Councilmembers and 26 field stones as the Japanese Councilmembers.

Bamboo, which is a giant grass, grows in South and Central America, the Far East and eastern U.S. and Mexico. Almost all the specimens here are found in Japan. Golden Bamboo, Black Stemmed Bamboo, Striped Sasa and Palmata are a sample of the more than 1,000 varieties of this diverse plant.

Tea and snacks are served on weekend afternoons from April through September near the garden's Lower House. Stine built this house in 1922 as the family' summer home. In front of this home is a Zen or Dry Garden, a simple arrangement of five large stones, a Shrine lantern, black pine and gravel, which is raked into patterns.

You can enjoy a picnic below Hakone's new Cultural Exchange Center, a shady spot to contemplate the timelessness of a garden.

Hakone Gardens & Cultural Center
21000 Big Basin Way, Saratoga
408/867-7653 or 408/741-4994
Mon.-Fri. 10-5; Sat. & Sun. 11-5
$3 parking charge on weekends;
Free on weekdays, contributions appreciated

❦ Saso Herb Gardens

"Sometimes the things we step on can be those that are most helpful," said Louis Saso on a tour of his beloved herb garden.

Louis and his wife, Virginia, grow one of the largest collections of culinary, medicinal and ornamental herbs on the west coast, all in compact beds surrounding their home in Saratoga. Herbs are more than beautiful to look at and delicious to smell. The benefits of these plants range from curing migraine headaches to spicing up sausage.

You can stop by the gardens and gift shop during their open hours. To get the most out of your visit, call ahead to make sure someone will be available to show you around and answer questions.

Even better, come for a free guided tour, offered once a month from May through September. Virginia and Louis take turns showing guests and amateur herbalists their gardens. Included are plantings based on the signs of the Zodiac, Chinese medicinal herbs and ornamental oreganos. They're happy to answer questions about growing particular herbs and how they are used for cooking or healing.

The Saso's have been growing herbs for more than 30 years. It started when Louis was working in the wholesale produce business. He became intrigued by the small potted herbs that sold along with his vegetables and fruits.

He began growing herbs as a hobby. With the resurgence of herbs in cooking and healing in the 1960s, Louis grew even more involved. Virginia became adept at culinary herbal use and creating dry flower arrangements with ornamental herbs. By 1974, they started their own retail herb business.

Today, they share their expertise with visitors on a tour for all five senses. You begin with a free sample of herbal tea, while relaxing in the shade of a sprawling 400-year-old oak tree. As you walk around, Virginia cuts pieces of herbs and passes them among the group to feel, smell or taste. Tips cover growing, harvesting and how the herb is used.

Two 12-foot-long beds are devoted to oregano. "It's more than just for pizza," Virginia said. Many of these are ornamental, perfect for dried flower arrangements. "The best oreganos for eating are Italian and Greek," she said, snipping off pieces for visitors to try.

There's good reason why many herbs are traditional favorites with certain foods. Sage, for example, helps in digesting fats, which is why it tastes so good in sausage and turkey stuffing.

Looking over all this herbal abundance is a carved wooden statue of St. Fiacre, standing in the hub of the Zodiac beds. A bishop offered Fiacre all the land he could till in one day. With his guardian angel's help, Fiacre tilled a great expanse of land. People came to him and were miraculously cured by the herbs Fiacre grew.

Herbal cures aren't limited to miracle-workers. One migraine sufferer tried every medical procedure available without success. Then he tried feverfew. Each day, he'd eat three leaves. Within two months, he noticed a difference. Today, he is virtually cured. He doesn't even have to eat the pungent-tasting feverfew leaves anymore to prevent the headaches.

Some herbs are natural pesticides. Garlic chives keep aphids away from roses. Pots of basil are used in France at sidewalk cafes to repel flies. Others attract hummingbirds to your garden, including the ornamental varieties of Saso's 50 sages.

In the Saso's gift shop, you can admire Virginia's dried flower wreaths, ornaments and bouquets and choose a favorite to purchase. You can even buy organically grown herbs here to give your garden the best start possible.

Saso Herb Gardens
14625 Fruitvale Ave., Saratoga
408/867-0307
Gardens and Gift Shop open Wed.-Sat. 9-2:30
Tours first Sunday of each month, May-Aug.
Free

UC Berkeley Botanical Garden

The 33-acre University of California Botanical Garden encompasses more than 10,000 species and varieties of plants from every continent except Antarctica. Tucked into the Berkeley hills well off the beaten path, this is the fifth largest collection of plants in the United States.

Since they are arranged according to their native region, from Australia to the Mediterranean, the garden is a microcosm of the Earth, itself. You can walk through a New World Desert, where some of the cacti tower above your head, then skip over a stream gurgling through a redwood forest, see insect-eating tropical plants in the fern house, then discover how roses are hybridized.

The garden's roots trail as far back as the 1890s. Six hundred types of California native trees and shrubs were collected and planted in the area of campus that is now the Moffitt Undergraduate Library. All were drought tolerant since no irrigation system was in place.

By 1895, the garden blossomed to seven acres and 1,500 species. It was transplanted to its present location in Strawberry Canyon in the 1920s, but still clings to its roots—about a third of the garden is devoted to California native plants, including several rare and endangered species.

One unusual plant community in the California section is a compact patch of a pygmy forest. Like Paul Bunyan, you can look down to the tops of trees that are 50 years old. The display explains how a unique geology creates these naturally miniaturized forests. Other California native plant communities range from fresh water marsh to chapparal.

One of the oldest and most striking sections of the garden is the new world desert with plantings dating back to the 1930s. Cacti from North and

Central America and the Andes grow here. Some are ten feet high.

In sharp contrast is the lush forest directly downhill, where the path crosses over the babbling Strawberry Creek. On one end of the creek, a waterfall cascades gracefully to the serene Japanese pool. Follow the creek down to the palms and cycads. Here you can cross the threshold into the tropics in the hot, humid greenhouse. Plants include taro from tropical Asia, African violets from Tanzania, a prayer plant from Brazil and Arabian coffee from east Africa.

Man's use of plants is best seen in the Asia Garden nearby. In the medicinal herb section, markers, in both English and oriental characters, describe how the plant is used. Coriander induces perspiration and relieves chicken pox and measles. Ginger helps alleviate the common cold, nausea and seafood poisoning. There's even an opium poppy growing here.

Most of these plants are "wild-collected." Botanists actually obtained the seeds and cuttings from the plant's native area. Data on location, habitat, collector and date of collection is kept for each specimen. If you come from one of the United States, you might see a wildflower from your county planted in the North American section.

The "Garden of Plants from Mankind" reminds you you're in Berkeley. If you climb up the steep hill beyond that, you'll be rewarded with an informative display on selective breeding and hybridization of old roses. On a clear day, you can glimpse the Bay and the Golden Gate Bridge on the horizon.

UC Berkeley Botanical Garden
Centennial Dr., above Berkeley campus
510/642-3343
Open daily 9-4:45, Wed. until 7 PM
Closed Christmas
Free, contributions appreciated

Luther Burbank & Kyoto Koi

The Luther Burbank Home and Gardens in Santa Rosa offers more than a beautiful place to stroll. It is a unique tribute to one of our nation's most prolific horticulturists, Luther Burbank.

Burbank brought more than 800 new varieties of plants into the world, including over 200 varieties of fruits, 25 vegetables, nuts, grains and hundreds of ornamental flowers. Two of his most famous creations are the Shasta Daisy, with pure white petals, and the kiwi fruit. As you explore the garden, you'll find many of the plants that grow on this earth thanks to Burbank, including Burbank potatoes and the spineless cactus. From April through October, you also can tour the home where Burbank lived from 1884 to 1906.

Born in Massachusetts on March 7, 1849, Burbank was brought up on a farm and received only elementary education. In 1871, he developed the Burbank potato and sold the rights for $150, enough money to finance his move to Santa Rosa.

Burbank dedicated himself to improving the quality of plants to increase the world's food supply. On this site and in nearby Sebastopol, his work gained world renown. He tested about 30,000 varieties of plants, which led to 113 new varieties of prunes and plums alone, including the kiwi.

Today, the shelter in the hub of the garden displays historical photographs capturing some of Burbank's famous visitors, including Thomas Edison and Henry Ford.

Plantings include Shasta daisies, raised beds with vegetables and fruits from Burbank's experiments, a Paradox walnut tree and his plumcot, which is a cross between an apricot and a plum.

The Cedar of Lebanon was planted by Burbank around the turn of the century. He spent many enjoyable moments in the shade of this tree. When he died in 1926, he was buried here.

The Kyoto Koi & Garden Center is a very different, garden spot a short drive away. More of a public park than retail nursery ambiance, Kyoto Koi specializes in bonsai and koi, a type of colorful carp.

As soon as you enter Kyoto Koi, you walk over a footbridge spanning a meandering stream. Large gold and ivory koi, some more than 50 years old, undulate through the waters below. You're welcome to feed the koi with meal from the nearby dispenser.

Follow the stream as it curves past a miniature forest of bonsai, then flows outdoors to a tranquil garden of winding paths, pagodas, sculpted trees and a splashing rock waterfall fountain.

Kyoto Koi has an extensive selection of bonsai, trees specially grown to be miniatures. California Junipers less than three feet high can be 200 to 350 years old, naturally dwarfed by conditions in the Mojave Mountains where they were collected.

Bonsai experts are much like sculptors in training the tress with wire to grow in certain aesthetic shapes. Everyday except Monday and Tuesday, you can watch an expert prune and shape bonsai on a demonstration stand. People from across the nation call Kyoto Koi to find the perfect piece. Many cost $1,000 and more, but bonsai isn't limited to wealthy collectors. Some are less than $10.

If you want to enhance your garden, large tanks in back of the nursery teem with all shapes and sizes of fish for sale, from a $2 goldfish to a $500 koi.

Luther Burbank Home & Gardens
corner Santa Rosa Ave. & Sonoma Ave, Santa Rosa
707/524-5445
Garden open daily, during daylight hours
Home open April-Oct., Wed.-Sun. 10-3:30
Garden Free; House Tour $1 Adults, under 12 Free

Kyoto Koi & Garden Center
2783 Guerneville Rd. (3 mi. w. of 101), Santa Rosa
707/575-9223
Open daily 9-5:30
Free

Ya-Ka-Ama & California Carnivores

To see some of the most unusual plants in the world, without sloshing through a bog, try California Carnivores. This greenhouse showcases a fascinating collection of insect-eating plants, from the ominous Venus flytrap to glittering Sundews.

Another intriguing garden is just around the corner. Ya-Ka-Ama Indian Education Center is dedicated to growing plants native to the area and to educating people about their traditional uses.

Both gardens are located on the backroads of the Russian River area, a popular summer weekend getaway. California Carnivores shares its lovely hilltop site with Mark West Vineyards, which offers wine tasting and a delightful picnic area.

California Carnivores is one of the largest private collections of carnivorous plants in the world on display to the public. Over 300 varieties add to the jungle-like feel of this compact greenhouse.

Grower Peter D'Amato has been cultivating carnivorous plants since he was 12 and general manager Marilee Maertz is equally devoted. They delight in showing visitors their unusual specimens.

Carnivorous plants have been cultivated for almost 300 years. In 1875, Charles Darwin first proved that certain plants do eat insects and small animals. Some prey is microscopic. Large carnivores in the jungle have been known to consume rats—but never a man.

The plants at California Carnivores range from bizarre to beautiful. Butterworts are particularly pretty. These are delicate-looking plants with vibrant flowers, much like small orchid blooms. Their flat, sticky leaves catch tiny prey, like whiteflies, which are digested for their mineral content.

Another attractive variety is the American Pitcher Plant. These make excellent flycatchers. You can place purple pitchers on a sunny windowsill or the slender trumpet species on your patio. The growers once counted 22 flies caught in one hour by a white trumpet on a sunny spring morning.

You can buy many of the different varieties of carnivorous plants to beautify and help de-bug your home and patio. Prices range from $4 to $50.

Just down the street is the Ya-Ka-Ama Indian Education Center. This is a working nursery and fledgling learning garden which may become one of the area's most interesting attractions.

This land has been everything from a Mexican rancho, to a ranch owned by actor Fred MacMurray, to a CIA listening post in the 1950s. In 1970, the land was considered surplus property. Young local Indians occupied it, just as their counterparts occupied Alcatraz, and reclaimed the land under an 1887 treaty.

Today, Ya-Ka-Ama, which means "Our Land" in the Kashaya Pomo language, is fulfilling its mission as a Native American learning center. An herb garden will be marked with their traditional medicinal and culinary uses. A circular shade house will feature a "roof" of interlocking, live willow branches. Gourds are grown for use in ceremonies. Classes are taught in the ex-CIA buildings.

The nursery offers an excellent selection of native plants and herbs, including their trademark chocolate peppermint, a delicious reminder of your excursion.

California Carnivores
at Mark West Vineyards, Forestville; from River Rd,
turn north on Healdsburg-Trenton Rd.
707/838-1630
Open daily April-Nov. 10-4 or by appt. in winter
Free

Ya-Ka-Ama Indian Education Center
6215 Eastside Rd., Forestville
707/887-1541
Mon.-Fri. 9-5; Sat.& Sun. 10-3
Free

Mendocino Botanical Gardens

It doesn't look like much from the outside, a rustic wooden garden shop sharing a parking lot with a roadside cafe, but this only makes what's beyond the garden gate even more impressive.

The Mendocino Coast Botanical Gardens is a surprising oasis of more than 3,000 varieties of native and cultivated plants in over 20 plant collections. You can stroll through a formal perennial garden, meander along a gurgling stream hemmed with fern-covered hills, study the strange growths near the bog and even discover a pioneer grave deep in the forest.

During the whale watching months of December and March, the Gardens offers an added plus— secluded benches perched along the cliffs overlooking the crashing surf and restless Pacific. Whales have been spotted as close as 100 yards off-shore.

Even if you don't see any behemoths of the deep, this is a spectacular setting. You can see fishing boats bobbing in the waves, smell the briny scent of seawater and listen for the mournful call of a foghorn above the roar of the surf.

The Mendocino Coast Botanical Gardens are planted and maintained by almost 100 dedicated volunteers. They rely exclusively on the financial support from admissions, donations, memberships and plant and garden store sales. Recently, the California State Coastal Conservancy voted unanimously to purchase a 35-acre parcel which will nearly quadruple the size of the Gardens from 12 to 47 acres.

Open year-round, this is truly "a garden for all seasons." In the summer, the perennial garden bursts with the color of alyssum, phlox, lilacs and hydrangeas.

The Heath collection is a palette of pastels. The cactus and succulent garden seem otherworldly in this rich, forested region. An open greenhouse holds a "standard reference collection" of living ivy. Dozens of the trailing green plants fill the tables and shelves.

Even in the midst of winter, you'll find colorful blooms and ornamental leaves in both the formal plantings and natural areas of the preserve. Fuchsias shine like rubies among the green. Huge hydrangeas dot the hillside. Delicate Australian Bluebell Creepers grow along the trail.

The Gardens are famous for their Rhododendrons, which explode with color in early Spring. Some bloom as early as January. The Rhododendron Dell peaks in April and May. More than 1,200 species of Rhododendron are known worldwide, exhibiting pink, white, mauve and yellow flowers.

At the end of the Canyon Rim Trail, a small sign directs you to the Pioneer Grave Site. Deep in an evergreen grove is a tiny, turn-of-the-century cemetery. Picket fences, once white but now weatherworn, enclose the graves. Anonymous wooden crosses mark the tombs.

One gravesite is hardly bigger than a cradle. On another grave marker, the crude lettering reads, "In Memory of Irene Parrish. Born Dec 24, 1900. Died Nov 12, 1902. Aged 1 yr 10 mo 19 days." The tidy cemetery is a pleasant but poignant reminder to take time to smell the roses.

Mendocino Coast Botanical Gardens
West side of Highway 1, just south of Fort Bragg
707/964-4352
Open daily 10-4
$5 Adults; $4 Seniors over 60;
$3 ages 13-17; under 12 Free

Notes

Alcatraz

They were the worst of the worst, the incorrigibles, the prisoners that other prisons couldn't handle. Infamous criminals like Al Capone, Machine Gun Kelly and Robert "the Birdman" Stroud did time on "the Rock." Their legends still attract thousands of visitors to Alcatraz each year— these days for a more temporary stay.

This fascinating excursion begins with a fun 10-minute ferry ride on the Red & White Fleet from San Francisco's Pier 41 to Alcatraz island. You can relax inside, protected from the elements, or brave the bracing breeze to take in the panoramic view of the city skyline, Golden Gate Bridge and Alcatraz island.

Once you reach Alcatraz, you're welcome to wander past the guards' residences, around the prison grounds and through the ghostly cell house, where displays capture the stories of the prison's most notorious inmates. Exhibit rooms illustrate the history of the island, the myths and reality of its years as a prison and the prisons of today.

Although it's best known for its prison years, the history of La Isla de las Alcatraces, the island of the pelicans, dates to the late 1840s. The gold rush brought a boom in commerce on the Bay. Ships needed protection from natural hazards and pirates, particularly confederates hoping to finance the Civil War. The Alcatraz lighthouse was completed in 1854 and Fort Alcatraz became the most heavily armed fortification on the west coast.

The fort's natural isolation was ideal for housing military prisoners. By the early 1930s gangster era, it evolved into the ultimate federal penitentiary. Prisoners generally did not begin nor end their incarceration here. They were sent here only when proven too unruly for other jails and returned to other prisons when deemed manageable again.

Al Capone arrived with the first group of prisoners at the new Alcatraz federal penitentiary. Once he arrived, he was just another number. Capone, and Machine Gun Kelly, became altar boys.

Many cells suffer the ravages of time and vandalism. Others are restored. They had little more than a small table and chair that folded down from the wall, a cot and a toilet. Step into a cell and imagine spending 18 hours a day behind bars for many hopeless years. On the superb cellhouse audiocassette tour, you can hear the Alcatraz story first-hand from the prisoners and guards who lived here ($3 Adults; $3 Seniors; $1 ages 5-11).

One cell recreates the "Escape from Alcatraz" immortalized in the Clint Eastwood movie. Brothers Clarence and John Anglin and Frank Morris chiseled holes through their cell walls into a utility corridor. To fool the guard, they created dummy heads with art supplies and hair from the barber shop, then tucked them into blankets as if they were sleeping.

The escapees made it to the roof, down the outside of the cell house and into the water. They were never seen again. Most believe they drowned in the Bay's freezing water and strong tides.

In the dining room, you can see tear gas canisters on the wall, to be used in case of a riot. The menu still shows the last meal served in Alcatraz before it was closed in 1963.

Frank Heaney, author of <u>Inside the Walls of Alcatraz</u>, was the prison's youngest correctional officer. The island was "thick with animosity, dread and despair," he recalled. Worst of all, inmates could see vibrant San Francisco as they walked from the recreation yard to prison jobs. "It was like holding water out to a thirsty man," said Heaney.

Alcatraz Island
Golden Gate National Recreation Area
415/546-2882 (ferry info)
415/556-0560 (park info)
Frequent daily departures; Schedule varies by season
Advance reservations strongly recommended
Without Cell House audio tour: $5.50 Adults;
$4.60 Seniors 62 and over; $3 ages 5-11

🐻 *Mission San Francisco de Asis*

With towering skyscrapers, perpetual traffic and more than 3 million people, it's hard to imagine the San Francisco area as wilderness. The Mission San Francisco de Asis, located in the heart of the city, is one of the few remnants of that era.

Popularly known as the Mission Dolores, this is the oldest intact building in San Francisco. It was completed in 1791. At the time, this was a remote outpost, the sixth mission established by Father Junipero Serra. The village of Yerba Buena, later called San Francisco, was not even founded until 44 years later.

Although badly damaged in the 1906 earthquake, the mission has been completely restored. You enter immediately into the cool, cavernous chapel, 114 feet long by 22 wide. Its four-foot-thick adobe walls effectively cut off the outside heat, sunlight and 20th-century noises.

The wooden confessional doors are to the left as you enter. Men stood or knelt in front of the priest for confession while women entered a side closet to confess through the opening.

The ceiling is unusual for a chapel, painted entirely in a type of Bargello-striped pattern with Native American dyes. The vegetable dyes created dark, rich hues of brown, tawny mauve and gray. The altar, too, features darker colors, a marbled gray-green and dark mauve highlighted with gold. The altar and its statues came from Mexico in the early 1800s and, besides the gold being renewed, they have remained unchanged for almost two centuries.

Just outside the chapel, historical prints depict mission life in the 1800s—undeveloped hills, few people. One scene captures an 1842 bullfight at the

Spanish mission. Another display illustrates the damage sustained by the 1906 quake.

In back of the chapel, a small museum showcases artifacts from the mission and San Francisco's first settlers. The original A-frame roof truss hangs on one wall. Immense pieces of timber are lashed together with rawhide, not nailed. In 1918, these wood trusses were reinforced with steel to protect against more quake damage. A window cut from the wall plaster reveals the adobe brick structure.

This room was once used as the mission's school. Artifacts include an 1860s slate scratched with barely legible chalk letters, a far cry from today's computers. Another case encloses an intricate silver ciboria, monstrance and missal stand. Unfortunately some of these are replicas. The originals were stolen in 1982 and never recovered.

The small, peaceful cemetery borders one side of the chapel. Originally, the cemetery was much larger, as the faithful have been buried here since the mission's earliest days. Their graves were marked with simple wooden crosses that deteriorated with time. In consolidating the cemetery, the unidentified bodies were placed in a common grave marked with a Lourdes shrine to the "Forgotten Dead."

Many of the existing markers are from those who died in the years following the gold rush. San Francisco was growing rapidly, from a village of fewer than 100 to a metropolis of well over 10,000. You may recognize some of the names, such as Don Luis Antonio Arguello, the first governor of Alta California under Mexican rule, and the Castro's. City streets have been named after these pioneers who were laid to rest at this church, the birthplace of San Francisco.

Mission San Francisco de Asis
16th and Dolores Sts., San Francisco
415/621-8203
Open daily 9-4
$1 contribution

San Jose Historical Museum

During a sunny midweek day, ladies in long skirts and wide-brimmed hats stroll past Victorian homes, peek into the doctor's office and drop by the imposing Empire Firehouse, where horse-drawn hook and ladder trucks await the next disaster. Most lead a boisterous brood of children, like old-fashioned schoolmarms on a class outing.

This is San Jose Historical Museum, a village of late 19th-century buildings relocated here from around the city, saved from the crush of ever-expanding development. Far removed from skyscrapers and silicon, the 25-acre museum is on the southern end of verdant Kelley Park, which also encompasses a small zoo and a Japanese Friendship Garden.

Clustered in this small town are the grand Pacific Hotel, founded in 1880, the 1862 Coyote Post Office and Dashaway Stables with its collection of high-toned riding carriages.

A favorite stop is O'Brien's Candy Store, once acclaimed as "the prettiest and most attractive candy store on the Pacific Coast." Founded in 1868 by an Irish immigrant, it was the first place to serve ice cream and sodas west of Detroit. Today, you can still enjoy an ice cream sundae in its old-fashioned soda shop setting.

The Candy Store is one of the shops on the ground floor of the Pacific Hotel. The hotel flourished in the late 19th century, advertised as "the most convenient house on the coast." For $1 to $1.50 per day for room and board, guests enjoyed a bar, bath, reading rooms, billiard halls and hardy German food.

The oddest structure in this village is a scaled-down replica of San Jose's Electric Light Tower.

The idea was to turn night into day downtown with one high and immense light.

On December 13, 1881, the 237-foot tower straddling Santa Clara and Market Streets was lighted, but the 24,000 candlepower beam proved a not-so-brilliant innovation. It didn't sufficiently light the area. By 1915, already damaged by a windstorm, the tower collapsed into the street.

The Umbarger and Chiechi Houses reflect the traditional family life of old San Jose. In the Umbarger's cozy, one-story, gingerbread, furnishings reveal the day-to-day lifestyle of the Victorian period—upright and refined.

The Chiechi House, which belonged to prominent orchardists, is furnished to reflect a later era. Children's games clutter the living room, a no-no in Victorian times. The kitchen features many newfangled electrical appliances, including a toaster, beaters and an ice box with a motor on top.

A peek into the dentist's office reveals the reason behind many people's fear of this profession. A nasty-looking drill hangs over the dentist's chair. Cuffs on the chair's arms kept squirming patients strapped in tight.

The rambling Stevens Ranch Fruit Barn recalls the area's major industry from the 1870s to 1940s. Orchards of prunes, apricots, plums and pears earned Santa Clara Valley the reputation as an international fruit production center. Once used for fruit drying, the barn now exhibits an excellent collection of historical photographs, antique fruit sorting bins and other artifacts.

Antique firefighting equipment is housed in the Empire Firehouse. The collection includes an 1808 hose truck with hand pump and the trampoline-style life saving system used to catch jumpers from tall buildings. A small park nearby offers a pleasant place to sit among San Jose's pioneer buildings.

San Jose Historic Museum
Kelley Park, at Senter and Phelan, San Jose
408/287-2290
Mon.-Fri. 10-4:30; Sat. & Sun. 12-4:30
$2 Adults; $1.50 Seniors 65 and over; $1 ages 6-17

🐻 *Carmel Mission*

More than two centuries ago, Father Junipero Serra raised a cross in the wilderness that we now call Carmel.

Today, a rough wooden cross stands in the very spot where the original was erected on August 24, 1771. Behind it rises the Mission San Carlos Borraneo del Rio Carmel, one of the most beautifully restored California missions.

Here you can see the graceful catenary arch of the chapel, the Moorish-style bell tower, period rooms depicting California's first library, a primitive kitchen and Serra's spartan bedroom as well as mission artifacts, richly embroidered vestments and the simple graveyard where Serra is buried.

The mission began as a crude log structure, a place to preach the word of Christ to the Indians. Wood buildings were replaced with more permanent adobe as Serra continued his journey along the California coast, founding nine more missions.

Serra would never see the present stone church that is the prize of the Carmel Mission. He died in 1784, nine years before its construction began. But near his quiet burial plot, his successor, Padre Lausen, fulfilled Serra's vision.

A colorful, Spanish-style garden leads to the graceful facade of the church. Two towers, one topped with a dome and a cross, frame its large wooden doors. Above the doors, a star-shaped window serves as focal point for the design.

This is actually a reconstruction of the original church. After Carmel was secularized in 1834, the mission was gradually abandoned and fell into decay and ruin. Photos just inside the entrance reveal the disastrous state of the mission. Complete restoration began in 1931, bringing the church and its environs back to their original state.

Built of native sandstone, the church's interior walls curve inward forming a graceful seamless arch overhead. The altar is painted in rich burgundy and deep sea green tones. On the rear balcony, a large pipe organ reaches for the ceiling.

Allow time to wander through the smaller adobe rooms of the mission. One display shines with intricate gold and silver altar pieces Serra brought from Mexico in the 1770s. Another room holds richly embroidered vestments from the 1780s to 1800s. The finely crafted white lace was made by Indian girls who were taught by the Spanish soldiers' wives.

The Carmel Mission was home to California's first library. It began with 30 volumes acquired from Mexico City's Apolistic College in 1778. One period room recreates the small library. Worn leather volumes crowd the shelves surrounding a sturdy desk topped with a candle and hourglass.

In contrast with Serra's elaborate sarcophagus are his spartan sleeping quarters, furnished with little more than a crude bed. Another room recreates the mission's kitchen complete with beehive oven and cords of garlic dangling from the ceiling.

The courtyard is the most peaceful place in the mission, with soft Wisteria hanging from its walls and a pleasant fountain splashing in its center. A smaller courtyard encompasses graves outlined with abalone shells and marked with small wooden crosses.

One gravestone commemorates "Old Gabriel," who died on March 14, 1890, "Aged 151 years." Church records show that Gabriel was not so long-lived, however, leaving this life at a spry 119 years old.

Take your time wandering through the Carmel Mission to enjoy its tranquil gardens and get a feel for this slice of old California and life at one of its most graceful missions.

Carmel Mission
Rio Rd. and Lausen Dr., Carmel
408/624-3600
Mon.-Sat. 9:30-4:30; Sun. 10:30-4:30
$1 Donation requested

🐻 *Wilder Ranch State Park*

In 1896 the local paper called Wilder Ranch "the cream dairy of the county and one of the finest in California," In its extra long cow barn, 206 cows were milked twice a day. The Victorian horse barn sported four different types of shingles and five colors of paint. The farmhouse was not only one of the first in the county to get electricity, but it had innovative lights that turned on automatically when the closet door was opened.

Today, the cows and horses are gone, but not much else has changed. This is a time capsule of a turn-of-the-century California dairy farm. The milking barn, horse barn, Victorian farmhouses, machine shops and eight other ranch buildings have been preserved as Wilder Ranch State Park, about two miles north of Santa Cruz.

Nestled in a valley with acres of rolling fields stretching to the coast, the ranch's white buildings seem to glow with the past. On weekends, costumed docents add to the authenticity by demonstrating traditional ranchwork, such as blacksmithing or butter churning.

The oldest building on the ranch is the weathered, circa 1839 Bolcoff Adobe. Bolcoff, a Russian sailor who jumped ship in Monterey and later married a wealthy Mexican woman, first started a butter and cheese dairy here.

By the 1850s, a man named Moses Meder owned the ranch. Meder had been a ship's carpenter and it's believed that he built the east coast Gothic-style Victorian farmhouse himself. It is the fanciest building on the ranch even today.

The farm grew into a major dairy operation 20 years later under a new owner, Levi K. Baldwin, a dairyman from Marin, and his partner, Deloss D. Wilder. Each day, they churned 300 pounds of butter by horsepower and shipped it north to San Francisco.

Wilder introduced a major innovation to his dairy business by installing Pelton water wheels. Turned by water pressure and connected by belts and pulleys to various machines, these wheels powered saws, drills, lathes, even a coffee grinder. Today, with a turn of a faucet, docents put the actual Pelton wheel back to work in the machine shop.

The other large farmhouse on the property was built for Deloss' son, Melvin D. Wilder, the engineer of the family. The home has been authentically renovated to reflect that era. The kitchen holds the original massive cast iron stove. Redwood paneling has been false-grained to look like oak, a popular style at the time.

When you open the dining room closet door, Melvin's inventive light automatically turns on and you discover the Wilder family's growth chart on the back of the door. In the living room fireplace hearth is a tile bearing the likeness of former president McKinley. Melvin was a staunch Republican.

You also can explore the garage, with its 1930 Model A Ford and 1916 Dodge touring sedan. In the horse barn, look for the innovative shoots where hay was sent directly from the loft to each stall. The visitor center tells the story of the ranch with historical photographs, newspaper clippings and dairy farm artifacts. When you stroll around Wilder Ranch State Park, you easily can imagine that you're visiting a dairy farm of 100 years past.

Wilder Ranch State Park
Along Highway 1, two miles north of Santa Cruz
408/426-0505
Open daily 10-4 (Call first. Hours may vary.)
$6 per vehicle day use fee: $5 if senior is in car
Includes same-day admission
to other state parks and beaches

🐻 *Ardenwood Historic Farm*

There are few places where you actually relive history. Ardenwood Historic Farm is one of them. You can help harvest wheat and other crops using vintage tools, ride on a horse-powered railroad, tour a Victorian farm house, taste home-made jam with biscuits baked in an old-fashioned oven, watch a blacksmith work and much more.

This 205-acre treasure is located just east of the Dumbarton Bridge in Fremont. Follow the signs down a narrow country lane. As you drive by the bountiful vegetable fields, you head further into the past until you reach Ardenwood and the late 1800s.

A graceful, gleaming white Victorian is the hub of the farm. This was the home of George and Clara Patterson, the land's original settlers. Patterson came west in 1849 to join the gold rush, but a year and a half of mining left him ill and broke. He realized the real fortune lay in what he knew best—farming.

After working for farmers near Mission San Jose, he was able to acquire nearly 6,000 acres of land, becoming one of the wealthiest men in the area.

The elaborate Queen Anne addition of this house was built in 1889 by renowned architect Samuel Newsom. It features a two-story turret, arched porticos and stained glass windows.

Exotic woods highlight the interior. In the double foyers, sycamore archways echo a Turkish influence in vogue at the time. The mantel in the guest parlor is carved mahogany. The pocket door has a veneer of burled redwood.

Period furnishings set the mood throughout the home. Upstairs, you can feel the unusual horsehair mattress on George and Clara's elaborate wood bed. The kitchen is full of gadgets from the early 1900s, including a vintage butter churner, bread kneader, cherry pitter, hot water heater and 1911 stove still used today.

Patterson fought an ongoing battle with the railroad, who wanted a right-of-way across his land. When he returned from his honeymoon, he found that the railroad had laid the track in his absence. After he successfully sued, the railroad had to stop on demand for the Pattersons. They had their own private depot.

Today, you can ride on a horse-powered railroad around Ardenwood. There's also a haywagon pulled by a brother and sister team of 2,000-pound Belgian draft horses. It winds past crops that Patterson grew here 100 years ago.

Special programs are offered throughout the seasons. During wheat harvest in August, volunteers are handed old-fashioned wooden pitchforks to heave bundles of wheat onto the wagon. Then, you watch as the 1920s thresher separates the wheat berry from the chaff. The berries are then ground into flour. You can sample a taste of your hard work in the biscuits cooked in the wood-fueled oven.

Special programs include jam-making, story telling and animal feeding. Kids especially enjoy visiting the farm animals. You'll see sheep, goats, pigs, turkeys and chickens. They'll also surprise you by wanting to do the laundry, using a hand-powered agitator and wringer. A snack shop offers vintage foods for sale, including scrapple and fudge.

Come to Ardenwood early. The Patterson House tours are offered on a first-come, first served basis and can sell out. Children under 6 are not allowed on the House tours, but there is plenty of fun here for the whole family.

Ardenwood Historic Farm
34600 Ardenwood Blvd., Fremont
510/796-0663 (recording)
Open April-Nov., Th.-Sun. 10-5
Also open public holidays and first weekend in Dec.
$5 Adults; $3 Seniors 62 and over; $2.50 ages 4-17
(includes haywagon and railway rides, house tour
and special programs)

🐻 *Camron-Stanford House*

Lifestyles of the rich and famous—in Oakland? Yes, in the 1870s. Lake Merritt was the playground of the Victorian elite. The Camron-Stanford house, overlooking the water, is a living reminder of that era, an intimate look at Oakland's heyday.

At one time, several stately Victorian homes ringed the lake. Each sported a carriage house, a boathouse and a boat.

Built in 1876, the Camron-Stanford House was not the grandest, largest nor most expensive. Nevertheless, it boasts an elaborate exterior and interior, which has been lovingly restored by historic-minded preservationists.

The home is a large four-story structure, its ground floor patterned with arched Italianate windows. As in most Victorian homes, it is highlighted with graceful and intricate details. Columns topped with lotus-motif capitals frame the front door. A delicate pattern is etched into the door's glass panels. On the side door, one etched glass panel is a century old, the other a reproduction, but even close inspection won't reveal the difference.

Much of the home had to be restored after its long and varied history. In addition to Josiah Stanford, the man who introduced the champagne grape to California and the older brother to railroad baron Leland, four other families lived here. In 1907, the City of Oakland purchased the house and, after remodeling, used it as the Oakland Public Museum until 1967 when the new museum was built.

The Camron-Stanford House Preservation Association rallied to save the house from demolition. Using diaries, letters and newspaper accounts, they restored the home to the time when the David Hewes family lived here, from 1877 to 1881.

The best way to start your tour is by watching "Living In a House." This award-winning slide show combines the colorful letters of Franklina Gray Bartlett, Hewes' stepdaughter, and vintage photographs to relate the history of three generations. It is a telling illustration of how changing lifestyles are reflected in home furnishings and decorations.

In the hall, there is a pump organ and an ornate statuary cabinet patterned with inlaid wood. The three-legged gypsy table, like all the tables in the home, is covered with a cloth, proof that the Victorians didn't like bareness in anything.

Some of the elaborate flower arrangements, seashell picture frames and other crafts were created by the lady of the house, which not only showed artistic talent but that they were wealthy enough to have the leisure to do it.

In the formal parlor, the center table is covered with a soft paisley cloth, very chic at the time. The gas chandelier, or "gasolier," is one of two still working in Oakland. Lighting determined the arrangement of furniture. The table is in the center of the room to take advantage of the gasolier's light. When wall fixtures came into vogue, reading chairs and small tables were moved to a room's perimeter.

Throughout the house, patterns decorate the wall borders, carpets and ceiling medallions. Whether you look up, down or around, you will see flowing geometric shapes and unusual colors.

The exhibit room downstairs illustrates the stages of restoration through photographs, tools and cutaways of plaster and wood. You'll come away with a full appreciation of the energy Victorians devoted to their homes, and of the restorers who brought it back to life.

Camron-Stanford House
Oak and 14th Sts., Oakland
510/836-1976
Wed. 11-4; Sun. 1-5
$2 Adults; $1 Seniors 65 and over

Shadelands Ranch

If you want to see what the East Bay was like before high-tech office buildings, shopping malls and traffic congestion, visit the Shadelands Ranch Historical Museum in Walnut Creek. It is a provocative glimpse into the hard-working farmlife of the early 20th century.

Completed in 1903, this two-story Colonial Revival house was the home of Hiram Penniman, his wife, Carrie, and his unmarried daughter, Mary. At the time, it was surrounded by 320 acres of farmland, where Penniman raised pears, prunes and three different types of walnuts.

Originally from New York, Penniman came west for the gold rush, but he didn't pursue that for long. Like a lot of prospectors, he discovered the real gold was in agriculture. In 1854, Penniman and his brother-in-law squatted on this land. They eventually purchased it, creating the Shadelands Ranch.

Don't expect a frilly Victorian. The Shadelands home was a sturdy, practical farmhouse, something you might see in the midwest, with sunny bay windows and a wrap-around veranda. Even the door is exceptionally wide and solid-looking. Some say the extra width was the ultimate practicality—it accommodated caskets. At the time, the deceased were viewed in people's parlors. Another story claims that the extra wide door allowed for the Pennimans' heavy wood furniture.

Almost all of the furniture in the Shadelands Museum was in the home when the Pennimans lived here nearly 90 years ago. A true time capsule of that era, even the books, china and tablecloths belonged to the Pennimans.

In the dining room, the table is set with white china with gold leaf trim. An ornate wooden sideboard, featuring a carved wooden buck's head, holds odd pieces, including a pretty serving plate and an oblong teapot with a blue windmills and fishermen design from about the 1840s.

The parlor's wooden furniture includes an octagonal table and a heavy, gracefully carved writing desk. The unusual texture in these rooms' fireplaces are from "clinker bricks." These bricks are seconds, off-sized and mis-shaped.

A wide oak staircase rises majestically through the center of the house. On the landing, a window seat stretches beneath a row of sunny windows that once overlooked acres of walnuts.

Upstairs, the master bedroom has been transformed into the "History Room." Here, the Walnut Creek Historical Society preserves old maps, records and photographs of the area. On the wall, an aerial photograph shows how the town looked on September 13, 1928, one of the archives' estimated 1,000 pictures.

The second bedroom belonged to Mary, Penniman's unwed daughter. Many believe that Penniman, thinking Mary would remain a spinster, built this house for her.

A hall closet holds Bessie's wedding dress, Penniman's daughter from his second marriage. Bessie stayed in the third bedroom when she visited. Like the other bedrooms, it has its own closet and washroom with pumped water. The Shadelands was not without these modern amenities, including central heat.

The guest bedroom now showcases kitchen memorabilia from the Pennimans' time here, offering a homespun look at everyday life in the early 1900s. The collection includes a two-burner kerosene stove, a wooden icebox, tin bread and cake boxes, a large wicker baby carriage, an unusual hand-powered vacuum and more.

Shadelands Ranch Historical Museum
2660 Ygnacio Valley Rd., Walnut Creek
510/935-7871
Wed.-Th. 11:30-4; Sun. 1-4
$2 Adults; $1 Seniors; Children under 12 Free

🐻 *Treasure Island*

When San Francisco hosted the west coast's 1939 World's Fair, we celebrated on a grand scale. No ordinary fair, this was an 18-month jubilee of new deals, broadened horizons and futuristic technology—the Golden Gate International Exposition.

Even with economic depression, labor unrest and impending world war, nothing seemed far from the grasp of modern man. Travelers flew across the vast Pacific to Honolulu in an amazing 14 hours. Two grand bridges now spanned the San Francisco Bay.

Not just any stretch of land would do for the Exposition. From the depths of the San Francisco Bay, we created an island. It would stand near the center of the spanking new Bay Bridge. As the dredges scooped up decades of soil washed into the Bay from Sierra mines, flecks of gold gave the new land its name—Treasure Island.

Today, it is a quiet Navy base, far removed from the time when hundreds of thousand of visitors filled its shores. Although thousands of motorists speed by the island on their way to and from San Francisco, few stop to see what it's all about.

Those who do veer off the sharp Treasure Island exit will find a quiet, palm-lined island, one of the best and most easily accessible views of the San Francisco skyline and a small museum that capsules the history of our nation's military at sea.

The Navy, Marine Corps, Coast Guard Museum is in one of the few original buildings from the exposition. It is "Pacific Basin" style, a horse-shoe shaped structure with art deco details. The only other exposition-era structures are two hangars inaccessible to the general public, as is the rest of the island. The glory of the Exposition is long gone.

But before you explore the museum, imagine for a moment one of the building's original purposes. It was the West Coast China Clipper Terminal for Pan-

American Airways, the take-off point for destinations in the Far East. Twice a week during the exposition years, these propeller-driven "flying boats" landed in the water here. Fashionable ladies and Indiana Joneses embarked for adventures in exotic Asia.

The palms are some of the more than 4,000 trees lifted from California gardens and planted here, along with 800,000 annuals, 400,000 perennials and 250,000 tulips.

During its heyday, parades, cavalcades, pole-balancing acts, motorcycle cowgirls, comedians, presidents and maharajahs filled Treasure Island with an unmatched exuberance. Shows ranged from wholesome puppet theater to nude follies. Exhibits boasted of the transparent "phone of the future," robots and diesel automobile engines.

The Golden Gate International Exposition closed its doors on September 29, 1940. Soon the Tower of the Sun and Triumphal Arch were replaced with naval buildings. The exposition's celebration of the Pacific Basin fell to the War in the Pacific.

Find out more about our nation's military at sea in the museum. A 251-foot-long, 26-foot-high mural depicts some key eras of our naval history.

Exhibit highlights include uniforms from a Boxer Rebellion Marine to a Vietnam-era helicopter pilot, ship models and paintings. One exhibit illustrates how the military trained Navajos as "Code-Talkers." The Navajo language was so foreign to the Japanese that they were never able to break the code. Ask the docent to demonstrate the immense, working, circa-1854 Fresnel lighthouse lens from the Farallon Islands. One gallery is devoted to artifacts from the Exposition.

Next time you're speeding by Treasure Island, take a quick detour to discover this island in history.

Navy, Marine Corps, Coast Guard Museum
Treasure Island
415/395-5068
Open daily 10-3:30
Free

🐻 *Petaluma Adobe*

Sink your fingers into a sheep's full wool coat. Feel the velvet of a burro's ear. Peak into a beehive oven while listening to roosters crow and the gay strum of a Spanish guitar in the background. Maybe even watch candles being dipped into a huge iron cauldron with a skim of wax melted over a smoky wood fire.

You can enjoy these experiences and more at the Petaluma Adobe State Historic Park, one of the largest and best restored of California's Mexican-era adobes. Period furniture, a menagerie of livestock and authentic details recreate a typical day on the rancho of the 1830s and '40s.

This immense fortress of an adobe was once the center of activity for Mariano Guadalupe Vallejo's Petaluma Rancho, a sprawling 66,000-acre, 100-square-mile agricultural empire. The existing west wing alone is more than half a football field long.

Now it forms one side of a giant horseshoe-shaped, two-story building, with wide wooden verandas and balconies stretching completely around the structure. In its prime, it was twice as large, forming a quadrangle where more than 2,000 Indians worked.

The workers would feel right at home if they returned today. Whitewashed beehive ovens wait in the courtyard. Hides lay piled in the crude wooden oxcart, one of only three authentically recreated, working "carretas" in the state.

As you wander around, you will find a fully stocked indoor kitchen and a weaving room with looms, spinning wheels and brightly colored finished cloth hanging from the rafters. Further along, you'll see the fancy living quarters of Vallejo, the simple room of the rancho's majordomo and the comfortable guest room. Across the courtyard are a workshop and warehouse for the hide and tallow trade and more.

Hides and tallow, which was rendered from cattle fat to make soap and candles, were the rancho's main industry. They were traded for goods from the European, American and other foreign ships that plied the California coast. Some of these international goods are represented in Vallejo's parlor, including a marble-topped table, crystal stemware and fine wood writing desk.

The rancho's farms raised an abundance of wheat, barley, corn, beans and vegetables. Its weavers manufactured enough cloth and blankets for 2,000 Indians. Blacksmiths and tanneries were mini-factories, turning out finished nails, tools and ready-made leather for saddles. Vallejo became one of the richest men in California.

The empire fell to a sudden end when the Bear Flag Revolt of 1846 claimed California for America. The Indian workers ran away and looters and squatters cleaned out the rancho's holdings. In 1880, at 72 years old, Vallejo returned to look at his adobe, now in ruins. "I compare the old relic with myself," he wrote to his son. "Then Youth, strength, and riches; now Age, weakness and poverty."

Petaluma Adobe State Historic Park
Adobe Rd., Petaluma
707/762-4871
Open Wed.-Sun. 10-5
$2 Adults; $1 ages 6-17

Extra Tip...If you're planning to spend the day visiting the area's historic sites, $2 covers same-day admission to Vallejo's home in Sonoma, the Sonoma Mission (see "Sonoma" in the "Towns to Explore" chapter) and the Sonoma barracks museum.

China Camp State Park

It is more than a century old, the last of the bay's Chinese fishing villages. In the 1880s, China Camp was a bustling town of 500, with a schoolteacher, barber, two gardeners, a doctor and three general stores.

Today one man, Frank Quan, carries on the heritage of his ancestors. You can catch a glimpse of what their life was like by visiting China Camp State Park's historic village and museum.

Just north of the Richmond/San Rafael Bridge in Marin County, China Camp is an easy, sunny getaway. Hikers explore forested hills. Birdwatchers flock to the emerald-hued wetlands' duck blinds. Picnickers enjoy the tables overlooking the bay and the sandy beaches.

A winding road along the bay's shore leads to the weathered wooden buildings of China Camp. Only a few structures remain, including Frank Quan's simple home, a shrimp drying platform and a long pier jutting into the water. A decayed fishing boat rests on the beach.

One of the buildings has been converted to a nostalgic beach food stand. Another houses a small museum that tells the story of the bay's Chinese fishing villages through artifacts and historical photos.

Lured to California by gold, the Chinese found success in a more familiar endeavor—shrimp fishing. In the late 19th century, as many as 30 Chinese fishing villages, with their fishing junks and sampans, dotted the San Francisco and San Pablo Bays. The immigrants found peace from prejudice in their isolated communities, where they maintained their Chinese culture and spoke their native language.

The museum's small aquarium showcases the tiny shrimp that the Chinese caught in these waters. Most of the shrimp were dried and exported to China, up to one million pounds in a good year. In season, the hillsides were covered with drying shrimp.

One of the museum's wooden artifacts includes a five-foot-tall fan mill. Following a 2,000-year-old Chinese design, this mill crushed the dried shrimp and separated the shells from the meat. Other artifacts include barrels, nets and china rice bowls and soup spoons found on the site.

The Chinese shrimp export industry thrived until the late 1800s, when racial hostility heightened. In 1905, the export of dried shrimp was banned. In 1910, the season was closed during the best shrimping months. In 1911, a law prohibited bag nets and the possession of dried shrimp.

These laws effectively cut off any hope of the Chinese continuing their shrimp fishing. The villages slowly died out. By the 1930s, China Camp was the last of the Chinese fishing villages on the bay, operated by a sole family, the Quan's.

Frank Quan still fishes here. Most of his shrimp catch is sold as bait, but depending on the catch you may still be able to purchase fresh grass shrimp at the snack bar on weekends. It is said to be one of the tastiest shrimp in the world.

China Camp State Park
North of Richmond/San Rafael Bridge, Marin
Follow China Camp signs off 101 North
State Park open daily 8 A.M.-Sunset
Museum open daily 10-5
415/456-0766
Free

Fort Ross State Historic Park

Long before most American pioneers headed west to tame a new frontier, the Russians journeyed east to become some of California's first white settlers. Fort Ross is dedicated to preserving that fascinating, if short-lived, Russian pioneer era.

Perched on a rocky bluff above the Pacific coast north of Jenner, this is an authentic recreation of the original fort that stood on this site from 1812 to 1841. You can venture into an octagonal blockhouse complete with cannons, an armory with barrels of gun powder and rows of muskets, the officials' quarters with well-stocked kitchen and a traditional Russian Orthodox chapel.

Begin your tour of Fort Ross in the visitor center. Take time to review the exhibits that illustrate the history of the area, which present an intriguing picture of the peoples that lived here.

The Kashaya Pomo Indians had inhabited the area for centuries, living off the land and sea. The Russian founder of the fort, Ivan Alexandrovich Kuskov, arrived in 1812 with 25 fellow countrymen and 80 native Alaskans. They constructed a fort with the traditional stockade, blockhouses and log buildings like those in Siberia and Alaska.

The Russians came to hunt sea otter, a prized pelt in their cold homeland. The Alaskans were skilled hunters and expert fishermen, who brought 40 baidarkas with them for hunting. These are swift, maneuverable kayaks, an example of which is on display.

Before long, the supply of sea otters along this coast was exhausted. The managers of Fort Ross tried to establish a new industry in agriculture to supply Russian outposts in Alaska. This, too, proved unsuccessful. Despite developing such industries as brickmaking, timber products, milling, tanning, metalworking and three inland ranches, Fort Ross was losing money consistently.

In 1841, the Russians decided to abandon their colony on North America's western frontier. They sold the land to John Sutter, who moved the livestock, equipment and armaments to his fort of New Helvetia, which later became Sacramento.

Today, Fort Ross stands as though the Russians still live and work here. A tall, hand-hewn fence encircles the fort, with blockhouses towering above opposite corners. You can climb up to the blockhouse's second story and peak out past the cannons to a scene little changed over the years.

The Rotchev House is the only structure with original Russian materials. Although it is empty now, records show that this home of Fort Ross' last manager once held a "choice library, a piano, and a score of Mozart."

Spartan but adequate period furnishings decorate the rooms of the Officials' Quarters. Its iron workers' and carpenters' shops contain a small forge, tools and finished goods. The pantry is filled with a large brass samovar, barrels of peaches and potatoes and unplucked chickens and ducks hanging from hooks.

The armory in the Kuskov House also is well-stocked with barrels of powder and muskets. Other storerooms contain barrels marked in Russian, teapots, boots and fabrics. Upstairs, a scientist's lab showcases small animal skulls, pinecones and a primitive microscope.

The chapel is the most graceful building in the fort. The original was built in the mid-1820s and was the first Russian Orthodox structure on this continent outside Alaska.

After touring Fort Ross, you can walk out to the windy bluff and look back on what was once one of the loneliest settlements on the coast.

Fort Ross State Historic Park
Highway 1, 13 miles north of Jenner
707/847-3286
Open daily 10-4:30
$5 per car day use fee; $4 if senior is in car

🐻 *Sutter's Fort*

Who first cultivated California's central valley on a commercial scale? Whose enterprise led to the discovery of gold in the Sierra? Whose fledgling pioneer settlement evolved into our state capitol?

The answer is John Sutter. With little more than a dream, he set out to build an empire. He acquired 150,000 acres of land, herds of cattle and shipping, tanning and fishery industries. Ironically, his own logging operation would make his dream a nightmare, when it led to the discovery of gold.

Sutter's Fort State Historic Park in Sacramento recreates life in California before the gold rush and preserves Sutter's pioneering spirit.

The year is 1846, Sutter's dream is at its height. Whitewashed, ten-foot-tall adobe walls enclose an independent, self-contained community. As you walk around Sutter's Fort you will see a cooperage, textile mill, blacksmith, distillery, gunshop, bakery, trade store and living quarters.

Be sure to pick up a sound wand before you start your tour. Through it, you can hear the story of Sutter's Fort told by Sutter himself.

One exhibit room illustrates the history of the fort. The most striking display encases the doll that belonged to eight-year-old Patty Reed of the ill-fated Donner party. Originally headed for Sutter's Fort, the Donner party was trapped in the Sierra's winter snows. Many died; the others turned to cannibalism to survive.

Sutter welcomed all travelers to his fort and was well-known for his hospitality. Living quarters were spartan but adequate. One room in the fort recreates the Richey family's home, with a simple bed, cradle, spinning wheel and one small luxury, a pendant clock on the mantel.

In the blanket mill, a mannequin portraying a Native American woman works at a large spinning wheel. At one time, Sutter employed as many as

350 Indians. Some performed everyday tasks at the fort. He trained others as soldiers and vaqueros. Sutter constantly recruited citizens for his settlement, providing all who entered with food, clothing and shelter.

The kitchen, well-stocked with fireplaces and large iron pots, could feed up to 200 people a day. Usually about 50 were fed here. At least one or two steers were killed every day; during harvest, five or six were killed. Bread was baked in the beehive ovens in the courtyard.

The sawmill looks simple, but served an essential function at the fort. Almost everything, from doors and windows to cannon mounts, depended on craftsmen who knew how to use and shape different types of wood.

Lumber mills that provided this wood were an important facet of Sutter's empire. In 1847, he commissioned James Marshall to build a sawmill on land Sutter leased from the Coloma Indians. While building that mill, on January 24, 1848, Marshall discovered gold.

Sutter tried keeping the discovery a secret, but word leaked out. By May, many of Sutter's workers joined the rush. Skilled craftsmen left. Two-thirds of his wheat crop went unharvested.

Sutter could not protect his empire until the U.S. government officially recognized his Mexican land grants. By the time they did, in 1855, the squatters had settled in and could not be removed.

Ten years late, Sutter moved to Washington, DC in a last-ditch effort to gain compensation for his lost land from the U.S. government. He left California and his dream behind. After 14 years of fruitlessly struggling for retribution, Sutter died in a Washington hotel room on June 18, 1880.

Sutter's Fort State Historic Park
L St., between 26th & 28th, Sacramento
916/445-4422
Open daily 10-5,
except Thanksgiving, Dec. 25 & Jan. 1
$2 Adults; $1 ages 6-17

🐻 Columbia State Historic Park

Columbia is the best preserved gold rush town in California, a highlight of anyone's journey to the Mother Lode. Almost all the buildings in this 12-block section of town have been restored or authentically reconstructed. You can peek into a miner's cabin, enjoy a sasparilla in the saloon or buy gold panning supplies at the general store.

Costumed docents people the village, playing the roles of their counterparts from 140 years ago. The only mode of transportation is the Wells Fargo stagecoach—modern-day contraptions like the automobile are not allowed in this time capsule town.

The only sounds are the clip-clop of horses, the clang of the blacksmith's hammer and, perhaps, the tune of an old-time fiddler playing in the street on weekends.

Columbia was once the second largest town in California. It boasted four banks, eight hotels, 53 stores, three churches, 40 saloons and the largest gambling house in gold country. Like other towns in the Mother Lode, it was all built around gold.

Dr. Thaddeus Hildreth first found the precious yellow mineral here in March of 1850. Within three days, his party had gathered 45 pounds of gold. Within a month, 5,000 miners turned "Hildreth's Diggin's" into a boomtown of tents and shanties.

Buildings sprang up to house businesses serving the miners. And wealth started pouring in. An intricate water system, including a 60-mile-long aqueduct, was built to supply water for the placer mines. It's still used today.

People called Columbia "the Gem of the Southern Mines." The area yielded $87 million in gold. Today, you can see the scale that weighed $55 million of that fortune in the Wells Fargo office.

This elegant scale is so precise, it can measure the weight of a signature on a piece of paper.

You can relive the past with a ride on an authentic stagecoach. It comes thundering up to the Wells Fargo depot to let off and pick up passengers just like in the old west. You can even ride "shotgun" on the top of the stage next to the driver. ($4 Adults; $3.50 Seniors and ages 6-17; 50¢ more to ride shotgun.)

As you stroll down Main Street, you'll notice that many of the buildings, like the 1858 Wells Fargo office, are brick with iron shutters. Fire was always a problem in gold rush towns, and Columbia wasn't spared. An 1854 fire destroyed nearly the entire town. An 1857 fire burnt down all the wooden buildings. From then on, most buildings were made of brick with iron shutters as protection from fire.

Take a left down State Street to find Firehouse #1. Columbia's pride and joy is here—"Papeete," a bright red, gold-embossed, hand-pumped fire truck. Legend says that Papeete was originally made in Boston for the king of the Society Islands. (Papeete is the capital of Tahiti.) The machine arrived in San Francisco by sail, but the ship's crew rushed to the gold mines and abandoned it. Columbia bought it in 1859. Today, Papeete still shows off its stuff in the annual Fireman's Muster, held in May.

Many of the buildings house fun stores where you can buy antiques, toys or souvenirs. Peek into the City Hotel. Opened in 1856, it is restored to reflect its elegant heyday. Don't miss the museum with its excellent collection of gold rush artifacts.

For $3 to $5, you can even pan for gold in Columbia. Matlock Cabin, diagonally across from Wells Fargo, has a water trough seeded with real gold. Even if you don't strike it rich, you'll come home with golden memories of Columbia.

Columbia State Historic Park
Box 151, Columbia, CA 95310
209/532-4301
Open daily 10-4 year-round
Free

🐻 Donner Memorial State Park

It is a story of courage, tragedy, survival and just plain bad luck. Eighty-nine pioneers attempted to cross the Sierra Nevada mountains to California in 1846, but became trapped in one of the worst winters on record. Only 47 made it to the promised land, surviving on boiled ox hides, bones once thrown away as scraps and, ultimately, the bodies of those who succumbed.

At the Donner Memorial State Park near Truckee, a monument to these pioneers tells their story in more than words. The base of the monument, four times taller than the average person, marks the depth of the snow that winter. It is 22 feet high.

In the visitor center, you can learn more about the pioneers' journey in a provoking slide show. The center also features displays and artifacts that recount the history of our nation's westward emigration, from trailblazer Jebediah Smith to railroad baron Leland Stanford.

A self-guiding nature trail leads to the boulder that served as the back wall of the Murphy cabin. A plaque here lists the members of the ill-fated wagon train. Seven of the Donner family are listed under "Perished." The remaining seven Donners, mostly orphaned children, "Survived."

Like most pioneers, the Donners began their journey with high hopes of a new life in a bountiful land called California. A prosperous Illinois farm family, they started west with $10,000 sewn into a quilt and a few worldly goods in a covered wagon.

In Wyoming, an explorer, Lansford Hastings, recommended they try a new shortcut that would slice 350 miles off their route. The Donners, along with the Reeds, Murphys and several other families, decided to break away from the main wagon train and follow Hastings' directions.

That was their first mistake. Following the "shortcut," they had to hack a road out of 36 miles of wilderness, then cross 80 miles of desert, where they lost most of their oxen and cattle. By the time they rejoined the traditional route, they were three weeks behind the main wagon train.

Then they made their second mistake. Warned of a rough mountain crossing ahead, they rested near what is now Reno for a week. It was late October and snow started falling in the mountains, but they pushed on. They made it to Donner Lake, but could go no further through the ever-deepening snow drifts. Three attempts to cross the pass ended in snowbound defeat.

Trapped for the winter, they built shelters, but food was scarce. One by one, they died from starvation. The survivors resorted to eating the bodies of the deceased. The struggle continued for three cold months, until a rescue party reached them in late February.

The Donners' story is the most tragic of the pioneers' journeys, but the trail west led to hardship and endurance for all who travelled it. In the visitor center, a full-size covered wagon, with cooking pots, a simple prairie dress and water barrels, illustrates the crude lifestyle of the trail.

One display shows how wagons were dismantled and hauled with ropes up the steep, almost impassable hillsides. In another display, broken china pieces and beloved family heirlooms represent those left behind in desert sand after the oxen died and wagons were abandoned.

These are symbolic of the pioneers' battles, but Patty Reed, who was 8 years old when trapped here in 1846, told the lesson best: "Never take no cut-offs and hurry along as fast as you can."

Donner Memorial State Park
Off Highway 80, west of Truckee
916/587-3841
Open daily 10-4; closed Noon-1 for lunch in winter
$2 Adults; $1 ages 6-17

🐻 *Pioneer Yosemite History Center*

In the late 1800s, people came from throughout the west to see the natural marvels of what is now Yosemite National Park. Some decided to stay here. They were homesteaders, painters, cavalrymen, blacksmiths and bakers. Each carved out their place in Yosemite and in the Park's history.

The Pioneer Yosemite History Center in Wawona is a living tribute to the Park's pioneers. Century-old log buildings belonging to its first settlers were relocated here from around the Park in the 1950s and 1960s.

The buildings aren't open year-round, but visitors can peak into windows to see their rugged furnishings as they wander among them during the quieter off-season. During the summer, costumed docents enact the roles of Yosemite's pioneers.

A covered bridge reminiscent of Vermont is the gateway to this village-like setting. The bridge was built in 1857 by Galen Clark, Yosemite's first guardian. All Yosemite-bound traffic crossed it. The bridge was covered by the Washburn brothers, a family of ardent entrepreneurs who took over the Wawona hospitality business.

The Anderson building was winter home to George Anderson, one of the original tourist guides to Yosemite's wonders in the late 1800s. In 1875, Anderson was the first man to climb Half Dome.

Homesteaders claimed their piece of Yosemite. The home here was built in 1879 by the Hodgdons, ranchers from the San Joaquin Valley. Originally, this 2-story log building was located in Aspen Valley, near Crane Flat, where the Hodgdon's grazed cattle in the summer.

Damage caused by cattle and sheep grazing spurred John Muir and other preservationists to petition the government demanding protection of the land. Yosemite National Park was established in 1890, ending grazing in the high country.

The name Degnan is still seen on many of Yosemite's food services. In this bakery building, Bridget Degnan began selling bread in the 1880s at 12 1/2 cents per loaf. As travel to Yosemite increased, the demand for her bread grew. An oven capable of baking 50 loaves a day was used until 1900, when the permanent brick oven, taking up nearly half of this building, was installed.

At the turn of the century, visitors travelled by horseback and horse-drawn stage to the Valley. The trip from Wawona took 8 hours and stages had to change their 4-horse teams four times during the strenuous journey. Blacksmith shops, like the one here, were located throughout the park.

With the influx of visitors came the need for more security. In the early years, the U.S. Cavalry handled the job. Each summer, 150 troopers from San Francisco came to patrol trails, stock fish and enforce the no grazing and hunting regulations.

By 1914, the cavalry was replaced by Rangers, who had a new problem to deal with—automobiles. Buildings such as this Ranger Patrol station were used as automobile checkpoints. Drivers stopped here to pay the Park fee—$5 in 1915, the same price as today.

While in the Wawona area, hardy hikers will enjoy the trail to Chilnualna Falls—one of Yosemite's prettiest cascades. To reach the trail head, follow Chilnualna Falls Road. Just before the pavement ends, bear left. The trail begins immediately on your right. This is a steep path but the waterfall is not very far in. The trail continues to climb through picturesque woods to panoramic views.

Pioneer Yosemite History Center
Wawona, Yosemite National Park
209/375-6391 or 209/372-0265
Center open daily year-round;
Buildings open late June-Labor Day
Free with $5 per car Yosemite National Park fee

Notes

♠ *East Bay Parks*

You could spend a year of weekends exploring the Bay Area's many fine parks. For starters, these three diverse parks in the East Bay are perfect for a nearby getaway, romantic retreat or family outing.

Along with scenic trails, Black Diamond Mines Regional Park in Antioch is the setting for California's intriguing coal mining history.

Briones Regional Park in central Contra Costa County encompasses more than 5,300 acres of rolling ranchland, panoramic views, forested trails and picnic grounds.

Point Pinole Regional Shoreline is a surprising oasis hidden amidst the industrial development along the San Pablo Bay. Here you can hike and picnic along the shore, fish from a pier, and perhaps even stumble upon the grass-covered mounds that were, at one time, bunkers for the dynamite plant.

Black Diamond Mines is the furthest east of these parks. While you walk along the quiet trails of this more than 4,000-acre park today, it's hard to imagine that a thriving community once existed here.

From the 1860s to the turn of the century, this area boasted the largest coal mining operation in California. Nearly four million tons of "black diamonds" were removed. They supplied the pivotal fuel as the state moved from an agrarian economy through the Industrial Revolution.

By the 1920s, the coal mining operations had shut down due to rising production costs and the use of new energy sources. Over the next 30 years, 1,800,000 tons of sand were mined here. It was made into glass in Oakland and used for steel casting in Pittsburg, until these industries closed down.

Today, you can see a remnant of the area's history at the Rose Hill Cemetery, a short walk from the Somersville Road entrance. Weathered stones mark the graves of children who died in epidemics, women who died in childbirth and men who died in mining disasters. Some are marked in Welsh, the native country of many of the miners. From here, 34 miles of hiking trails wander past grassland, foothill woodland, chaparral and stream vegetation.

Briones Regional Park harkens back to the Mexican era when Felipe Briones had a cattle ranch here in 1829. Today, cattle still graze in the meadows of Briones. The park also is popular with horseback riders and offers spacious picnic areas.

Trails follow streams and climb up past bay laurel and buckeye trees to panoramic views of the surrounding area. This expansive park has entrances on all four sides, making it a nearby getaway from Lafayette, Pleasant Hill, Martinez and Berkeley.

Point Pinole Regional Shoreline is a hidden gem on the San Pablo Bay shore. Picnic tables and a play area are perched on a bluff above the water, a short walk from the parking lot. From here, trails lead to salt marshes, grassland and eucalyptus woodland.

For $.50 ($.25 for kids 6-11), a shuttle bus carries fishermen and picnickers to the 1,225-foot pier in the northern section of the park. From here you can dangle a line or just sit and watch the freight ships, tankers and sailboats cruise by.

Black Diamond Mines Regional Park
South end of Somersville Rd., Antioch
510/757-2620
Open daily 8 A.M.-dusk
Free

Briones Regional Park
Central Contra Costa County
510/531-9300
Open daily 8 A.M.-10 P.M. March-Sept.
(Alhambra entrance closes at dusk Oct.-Feb.)
$2.50 Parking Fee

Point Pinole Regional Park
From San Pablo Ave., follow Atlas Rd. to water
510/531-9300
Open daily 7 A.M.-8 P.M. in summer
Open daily 7 A.M.-6 P.M. in winter
Call for pier and shuttle hours
$2.50 Parking Fee

🌲 *Marin Headlands*

San Francisco is one of the few metropolitan areas in the country that is blessed with the stunning beauty of places like Marin Headlands. With the San Francisco skyline glimmering across the water, nature rules here with its rugged cliffs, mighty surf and soaring hawks.

In this surprising park, you can hike scenic trails, explore World War II batteries, visit a NIKE missile site, tour a lonesome lighthouse, see marine mammals being nursed back to health, search for agates on the beach, even stay overnight in a hostel. Be sure to call ahead for special ranger-led tours of the restricted areas, such as the lighthouse and missile site.

The Marin Headlands, an extension of the Golden Gate National Recreation Area, lies just northwest of the Golden Gate Bridge. The road along the shore offers an unbeatable close-up view of the graceful Golden Gate Bridge, but it is not for the faint of heart. Heading west, it becomes one-way, with steep curves and fatal drop-offs.

As you near the open Pacific, military relics become more prevalent. The tunnel-like Battery Wallace was first used in 1919 as an opening firing platform. The 12-inch guns here could duel with ships 17 miles out to sea. During World War II, the battery was covered with an earth shelter for fear of aerial attacks. By 1948, it was obsolete and shut down.

Displays along the road explain how the headlands was used for several generations of defense, from the Spanish-American to the Cold Wars, from mortars to disappearing guns. On certain days, you can visit the only NIKE missile site still preserved in the United States.

Point Bonita and its lonesome lighthouse stand on the western tip of the headlands, the threshold of the slim channel of water called the Golden Gate.

Until 1775, explorers sailed past and missed this narrow opening to the San Francisco Bay. From the open ocean, it appears as a continuous coastline.

During the gold rush of 1849, 775 vessels sailed through the Golden Gate. An historic photo on the display near the lighthouse shows San Francisco Bay as a forest of masts. But the rugged coastline became a graveyard of ships.

The Point Bonita Lighthouse was installed in 1855 to help guide vessels through the merciless waters. The original glass lens has been in continuous use since then. The lighthouse is reached by a tunnel dug by hand through the hillside.

You can visit injured elephant seals, sea lions and harbor seals being nursed back to health at the Marine Mammal Center (tel. 415/289-SEAL). The Headlands also is one of the best spots in the Bay Area to watch hawks. The migration begins in late August and peaks with several hundred sightings a day in late September. The best viewing point is the aptly named Hawk Hill.

Enjoy a day on the seashore at Rodeo Beach or search for agates at nearby Rodeo Lagoon. And if you don't want to rush home at night, you can stay in the Golden Gate Hostel (tel. 415/331-2777). Dormitory accommodations are available to guests of any age at $8 per night. The spacious hostel has a complete kitchen, comfortable living room with fireplace, ping pong and pool tables and company from all over the world with whom you can share your day's experience.

Marin Headlands
Northwest of the Golden Gate Bridge
From 101 North, take the Alexander Ave. exit
From 101 South, take the last Sausalito exit
Open 24 hours daily
415/331-1540
Free

♠ Muir Woods National Monument

Coast Redwoods are the tallest living things known to man. There is only one place on Earth where these trees grow—in scattered groves along just 500 miles of the Pacific coast from southern Oregon to San Luis Obispo County, California.

People from around the world journey to Muir Woods National Monument to walk among these awe-inspiring giants. This is one of the most magnificent and accessible of the Coast Redwood groves, located just an hour's scenic drive north of San Francisco.

Coast Redwoods in this forest tower more than 25 stories into the sky. Although this park is popular, crowds appear subdued next to these massive trees.

Paved, easy loop trails meander along Redwood Creek past several of Muir Woods' most spectacular groves. Hardy hikers can find solitude in the forest by following the steeper paths up the wooded canyon. Several trails eventually connect to Mt. Tamalpais State Park offering hours of quiet hiking.

As you enter Muir Woods National Monument, take a look at the cross-section of a Redwood trunk. It reveals hundreds of tree rings—one for each year of the tree's life. Dates are marked on certain rings to show how the tree grew silently and steadily upward while the civilization of man developed in the far corners of the world.

Most of the mature trees in Muir Woods are between 600 and 800 years old. The grove's oldest redwood is at least 1,000 years old. Until the 1800s, Coast Redwoods like these covered many northern California coastal valleys. Many of them fell to the logger's axe.

The grove at Muir Woods was spared because it was in a deep canyon that hampered accessibility. In

1905, recognizing that it was one of the Bay Area's last uncut stands of old-growth redwood, Congressman William Kent bought 295 acres and donated the land to the federal government. In 1908 President Theodore Roosevelt declared it a national monument. Kent requested it be named after famous conservationist John Muir.

The tallest trees in Muir Woods today are in the Cathedral and Bohemian Groves, easily reached by the paved trail along the stream. The tallest tree here stretches 254 feet high; the thickest is nearly 13 feet in diameter.

The redwood bark alone is six to 12 inches thick. It insulates the tree against fire. Still, repeated fires can burn through the bark, exposing heartwood to dry rot. Subsequent fires blacken the cavities that you see at the base of many trees in Muir Woods.

For 150 years, fires were suppressed to protect the forest. Now it's known that fire is essential to the forest's ecosystem. One benefit is that it clears the forest floor so that redwood seeds have a chance to reach soil and sprout.

Most of the redwoods reproduce by burl sprouting. The tight clusters of trees you see probably began as sprouts on the burl at the base of an established tree. As you walk through the woods, you can see these burl sprouts at different stages of development.

Coast redwoods aren't the only living things you'll see here. Other trees included the Douglas fir, maple, oak and laurel. Often deer forage near Redwood Creek in the early morning or at dusk. A popular bird with the kids is the bright blue Stellar's jay. The forest floor is carpeted with ferns and Redwood sorrel. Each season offers something special so if you haven't been to Muir Woods, go now. If you have visited, go again.

Muir Woods National Monument
Muir Woods exit off 101, Marin County
415/388-2595 (recording)
Open daily 8 A.M.-Sunset
Free, donations appreciated

🌲 *Point Reyes National Seashore*

It exploded with the force of 15,000,000 tons of TNT. It destroyed an entire city. And you are standing where it all began, at the 1906 earthquake's epicenter, when you walk along the self-guiding Earthquake Trail at Point Reyes National Seashore, about an hour's drive north of San Francisco.

This half-mile, wheelchair-accessible loop that teeters on the San Andreas Fault illustrates the history and future of a land in motion—the California coast. You can learn first-hand when to expect The Big One and still have plenty of time to explore the Point Reyes peninsula before it becomes an island.

Begin at the Bear Valley Visitor Center. It has excellent dioramas of sea and land animals in their natural habitats, Miwok Indian artifacts, displays recounting the first settlers and numerous shipwrecks, even a whale's skull. Near the seismographs, records of recent earthquakes, marked with their epicenters and strengths on the Richter scale, are evidence of the land's instability.

If you're still willing to walk along the active San Andreas Fault, cross the Bear Valley picnic area to the start of the Earthquake Trail, just to the left of the restrooms.

Along the trail, a line of blue posts marks the exact position of the San Andreas Fault. You are now standing on land that lurched 16 feet northward on April 18, 1906. The barn to your left moved along with the land, splitting from its foundation. Legend claims that this was near the spot where an unfortunate cow named Matilda met her demise. According to one story of the fateful day in 1906, the earth yawned open and swallowed her whole.

As you follow the trail, the line of blue posts bisects a fence. Here, it's easy to visualize the theory of plate tectonics explained in the trail's displays. The fence is split 16 feet apart. Half stands on one side of the Fault, on the Pacific plate; the other half stands on the other side of the Fault, on the American plate.

If you could remain in one spot in front of the park's visitor center for millions of years, you could see the land in motion. In a half-million years, the Center would become waterfront property as the Point Reyes peninsula, along with Los Angeles, breaks away from the continental U.S. and drifts northward. In 13 million years, the Center becomes a suburb of Los Angeles. In 40 million years, Point Reyes slides into the Aleutian Trench near Alaska.

Back in the 1990s, you have the rest of the day to explore Point Reyes. Near the Visitor Center, a recreation of a Miwok Indian Village presents a picture of the area before the white man. You can explore the underground Lammas, or ceremonial dance houses, and peek into the teepee-like Kotca huts. Every detail is authentic.

A 45-minute drive takes you over rolling, pastoral countryside and past dairy farms to the ocean. A half-mile walk further will bring you to the historic Point Reyes Lighthouse, which first guided ships in 1870 and was in service for more than a century before being retired.

The Seashore also encompasses many hiking trails, backpacking camps and excellent bird-watching spots. In the northern end of the park, you'll find an historic dairy farm and may catch a glimpse of the Seashore's free-roaming herd of tule elk near the more remote trails. Plan on spending a full day to explore Point Reyes. You only have half a million years before it breaks off and drifts away.

Point Reyes National Seashore
Off Highway 1, Marin County
415/663-1092
Seashore open 24 hours daily
Visitor Center open daily 9-5, weekends and
holidays 8-5; closed Christmas
Free

Richardson Bay Audubon Center

Just outside of Tiburon, the 900-acre Richardson Bay Audubon Center and Sanctuary showcases Marin's natural beauty, before condominiums conquered these quiet shores. It is an ideal spot for a short country walk, especially during bird watching season.

From October through April, migrating birds settle for the winter in the gentle waters and grassy hilltops of the Sanctuary. Autumn leaves carpet the path by the pond. The graceful Lyford house, an 1876 Victorian, is open for public tours on Sunday afternoons from November through April.

The Lyford House is perched on a small, tree-shaded bluff, just above the lapping waves of Richardson Bay with a view of the San Francisco skyline on the far horizon.

The house seems custom-made for this setting, but it was not built here. It originally stood on Strawberry Point, a half-mile across Richardson Bay, where Dr. Benjamin Lyford operated an "ultra-hygienic" dairy farm. Some thought Lyford was obsessed with cleanliness for advocating such ideas as chemical septic tanks and city sewage systems. By employing these healthful living theories at the dairy, Lyford could claim that his Jersey cows produced the healthiest milk.

Lyford died in 1906. His wife, Hilarita, passed on two years later, leaving no heirs. The Victorian home stood empty and abandoned. Suffering from years of neglect, it was scheduled for demolition in 1957 to make way for new development.

Rosie "the goat lady" Verrall came to its rescue. Since the age of three, Verrall lived on what is now the nature preserve. For years, her goats grazed on the lower slopes of the hills. To protect it from encroaching development, Verrall deeded this prime piece of real estate as a wildlife sanctuary. The Lyford House was loaded in one piece onto a barge and towed across Richardson Bay to its present location.

The 1/3-mile, self-guided nature trail begins just beyond the Lyford House. Be sure to borrow the booklet describing the plantlife and habitats along the trail. With it, you can distinguish a Laurel from a Live Oak and learn how Native Americans used the Soap Root plant to stupefy fish.

A gentle, uphill climb winds beneath three of California's most common trees: Coastal Live Oak, with prickly-edged leaves, California Bay, which emits a pungent odor when you rub its leaves, and Toyon, or California Holly, with bright red berries.

The top of the hill offers a lofty view of the area framing the San Francisco and Richardson Bays, including Angel Island, San Francisco, Sausalito and the coastal mountains.

The trail circles down the back of the hill. Ignore the freeway buzz in the distance and listen as the breeze whispers through the native bunch grasses. Near the bottom of the hill, you will hear seabirds as they float and fly across the inlet.

Walk along the back of the hill to find another distinct habitat in this small sanctuary. Woodland trees arch over the trail, providing a cool shade.

Veer off the main trail to the wooden bridge to your left. It crosses a small pond which attracts woodland and aquatic birds. This sidetrip also takes you to the compact garden devoted to California's native plants, a short walk from the parking lot.

Allow time to browse in the bookshop before you leave. It specializes in books on birds and gifts for bird lovers.

Richardson Bay Audubon Center
376 Greenwood Beach Rd., Tiburon
415/388-2524
Sanctuary open Wed.-Sun. 9-5 year-round
Lyford House open Sun. 1-4, first weekend in
Nov.-end of April,
Free; $2 donation suggested

🌲 *Pinnacles National Monument*

Wild pigs, pitch dark caves, towering rock spires, tarantulas—you don't have to travel far, or be Indiana Jones, to explore the exotic animal life and geologic formations of Pinnacles National Monument. This natural anomaly is located about three hours drive south of San Francisco, off Route 25 out of Gilroy and Hollister.

The east entrance to Pinnacles is the most popular starting point. Here, a visitor center features exhibits on the history of the park, its animal life and geological heritage.

The most striking aspect of Pinnacles is its sharp contrast to the land surrounding it. Rolling farmland suddenly gives way to craggy castles of rock, appearing like a strange island of stone towers.

This was once the insides of an 8,000-foot volcano. Twenty-three million years ago, this volcano lay 195 miles further south, east of what is now Los Angeles. Centered on the San Andreas rift zone, half the volcano lay on the Pacific Plate, the other half on the North American Plate.

The Pacific Plate migrated northward, carrying the west side of the immense volcano with it. Over the years, wind and rain eroded the rock into the turrets, peaks, spires and monuments that we now call the Pinnacles.

Pick up the 15-cent Moses Spring Self-guiding Trail brochure at the visitor center before embarking on this short, easy trail. It highlights the details that make Pinnacles unique. Without it, you might miss the gnarled red trunk of a manzanita, the lime green patches of lichens and the fertile oasis of chain ferns. Look for the Digger Pine's root which snakes through 26 feet of rock in its search for moisture.

You most likely will not miss the most pervasive wildlife in Pinnacles—rock climbers. With neon-colored ropes and the clang of carabiners, they seem to be scrambling up every rock tower along this trail. Almost everyone stops momentarily to watch them.

The Bear Gulch Caves are a favorite spot. Bring a flashlight and be aware that the caves are not for the claustrophobic. This is a narrow passage, completely cut off from outside light in several stretches, but a safe adventure for kids and adults.

Back in the 1870s, a notorious, murdering bandit named Vasquez used the caves as his hideout. Hotly pursued by a posse, he would ride into the Pinnacles and mysteriously disappear among the rocks. One legend claims that he stashed the loot from a nearby robbery in the caves before fleeing to Los Angeles. Shortly afterwards, he was apprehended and hung. The money was never found, but don't bother looking. Most believe the cache is a myth.

The High Peaks Trail is one of the most exciting trails in the park. A steep, winding climb brings you into, around and on top of the pinnacles. The trail is a legacy of the 1930s Civilian Conservation Corps. You can scramble up narrow steps carved out of sheer rock, then sidle beneath stony overhangs, the closest thing to rock climbing without a rope.

If you want to stay the night, a nicely landscaped, privately run campground is just outside the Pinnacles east entrance. Camping costs $6 per person per night, with a maximum of $24 charged per campsite. Facilities include a convenience store, showers, electrical hook-ups and group sites. For campground reservations and information, call 408/389-4462. There also is a small, walk-in campground located in Pinnacles on the west side of the park.

Pinnacles National Monument
101 to Gilroy, to Route 25 south,
to Route 146 west
408/389-4485
Park open 24 hours daily
Visitor Center open daily 9-5
$3 per vehicle, pass good for 7 days

Point Lobos State Reserve

It's been called "the greatest meeting of land and water in the world." This extravagant claim is close to the truth. Point Lobos preserves the best of California's coastline.

Short, easy trails lead to groves of Monterey Cypress, a colony of barking sea lions, otters cavorting in kelp beds, crashing waves and lively tide pools. The reserve is off Highway 1 just four miles south of Carmel.

Begin your visit at Whalers Cove. This is a popular launch point for SCUBA divers. These waters were declared the first underwater reserve in the U.S. in 1960 and access is strictly limited to protect the environment. From the parking lot, walk back up the road to Whaler's Cabin.

This weather-worn cabin was built around 1851, home to a family of Chinese fishermen. Today it is a museum which encapsulates the cove's history through photographs and fascinating artifacts.

Wooden buttons, a ceramic rice bowl and clay marbles were found when excavating the original dirt floor of the cabin. The wood floor that exists now was built near the turn of the century. A window cut into the floor planks reveals its unique support—a whale vertebra.

Whaling was the cove's main industry from 1862 to 1882. On the beach below this cabin, the Portuguese Whaling Company hauled in their harvest to render oil from the blubber.

An abalone cannery operated here from 1902 to 1933. The museum's two-man pump, resembling a railroad handcar, was used to pump air to the brave souls who worked underwater as helmet divers for abalone. Try picking up the heavy lead boots that held them to the bottom.

Another display shows a Monterey Jack cheese press and tells the story of the dairy on this land from 1903 to 1954. The cabin was used by the military during WWII when the cove was a training site for amphibious landing craft. Hollywood also discovered Point Lobos, shooting 34 films here, the first in 1919.

Today, Point Lobos is reserved for the natural treasure of land meeting sea. A number of trails explore the shoreline. Not far from the Whaler's Cabin, the Granite Point Trail winds around the cove far above the water.

Keep an eye out for harbor seals sunning themselves on the rocks below. Seals grow to about six feet long, are often gray or tan and usually sun on rocks close to the water.

To see and hear their larger cousins, the sea lions, drive to the Sea Lion Point parking lot. Follow the barking sounds down the reserve's most popular trail to the jut of land overlooking Sea Lion rocks. Point Lobos is named after these barking animals, a shortened version of its original description, "Punta de los Lobos Marinos," translated as "Point of the Sea Wolves."

Walk down one side of the overlook to the tidal pools near the crashing waves. Stay still for a moment and crabs and hermit crabs will appear from their rocky hiding places. Bright purple sea urchins squeeze into crevices.

Climb the trail to the point above the kelp beds. Look closely for sea otters in the kelp. From here, they resemble small logs. You may hear them "clapping" a shellfish open or see them looping in and out of the water.

After exploring Point Lobos, you may agree that it is "the greatest meeting of land and water in the world."

Point Lobos State Reserve
Off Highway 1; Four miles south of Carmel
408/624-4909
Open daily 9-dusk
$5 per car day use fee; $4 per car if senior is present

🌲 *Mariposa Grove of Big Trees*

They are not the oldest living things on earth. That distinction belongs to the bristle cone pine. They aren't even the tallest living things on earth. Those are the coastal redwoods. But Sequoiadendron giganteum, the giant Sequoia trees, are the largest living things, in sheer volume, known to man.

The Mariposa Grove of Big Trees is an awe-inspiring forest of giants. The Sequoias are thousands of years old and hundreds of feet tall. To get a feel for the size of these trees, here is an easy comparison. Take a friend who is 6 feet tall. Near his toe, place a twig that is 2 inches tall. The friend is the Sequoia. The twig is you.

This is just one of the comparisons that the park ranger may offer on an intriguing tour of this magnificent grove. Anyone who hasn't seen these trees might find it hard to believe. They wouldn't be alone.

In 1852, Mr. Dowd, a professional bear hunter, first stumbled upon the nearby Calaveras Big Trees. When he returned to camp with his stories of the immense forest, people figured it was simply a tall tale. He had to connive them into visiting the area by claiming he needed five men to help carry back the grizzly he shot.

Once the word was out, loggers came to this gold mine of lumber. They were soon disappointed. The Sequoias produced a brittle wood, often splintering when the tree fell. About 75% of the trees felled by the early loggers are still lying in the Mariposa Grove. The other 25% were made into vineyard stakes, shingles and matchsticks.

In 1864, Abraham Lincoln set aside Mariposa Grove as a state reserve. Eventually, it became part of Yosemite National Park.

The granddaddy of all the Sequoias in this grove is the Grizzly Giant. It's the oldest and largest living thing in Yosemite. This massive tree is 209 feet tall and 32 feet in diameter. Its age is estimated at 2,700 years. One of its limbs alone is almost 7 feet in diameter, larger than the trunk of any non-Sequoia in the grove.

It all began with a seed the size of an oat flake. These seeds are found in the Sequoia's cones, which are hardly bigger than a golf ball. Each cone contains about 200 seeds and each tree can produce 1,500 new cones each year. Some cones stay on the trees for as long as 22 years. You can count their rings just as in tree trunks.

Fire is essential to the growth of new Sequoias. The heat dries the cones high in the trees so that seeds can be dispersed by the wind. Flames clear the forest floor of undergrowth creating a bed for the seeds.

The Chickaree squirrel helps, too. When gathering food for the winter, the squirrel can bite 286 cones off the tree in 18 minutes. He eats the fleshy part of the cone, leaving the seeds to grow.

As the Sequoia grows taller, its roots spread outward, not deeper. During the growing season, they suck up about 1,000 gallons of water each day. Their roots are usually no deeper than 6 feet, but fan out to more 150 feet, creating a stable base for the towering tree.

Still, many Sequoias have fallen in this grove. When the tunnel tree fell, it could be heard in Fish Camp, five miles away. The immense trunks stretching across the forest floor provide another unique perspective on the world's largest living things.

Mariposa Grove of Big Trees
Yosemite National Park
209/372-0265
Open daily year-round, weather permitting
Free with $5 per car Yosemite National Park fee

🌲 *Yosemite Camera Walk & Other Freebies*

"It's not the camera that takes the picture. It's the photographer," James Johnson remarked as he led a group of amateur shutterbugs into Yosemite's meadows. "If there's one thing I'm going to teach you today, it's how to recognize a good photographic situation."

These free 90-minute camera walks are one of Yosemite's best bargains. They offer insights for visitors with pocket-sized, point-and-shoot cameras as well as enthusiasts with the three Nikons, a tripod and complete filter set. Group size is limited, so sign up in advance at the front desk of the Yosemite Lodge or the Ahwahnee. Walks are offered by the Photo Center and the Ansel Adams Center.

In the Photo Center, Johnson sees hundreds of pictures taken by visitors in Yosemite. Many share a common scene—and a common mistake. Friends and family pose in front of sun-soaked waterfalls and cliffs—except the people in the photo are too dark and the background is washed out. The camera, even an automatic, didn't know which exposure to use.

One solution is to make sure the people in your pictures are not in the shade. Another is to use a flash, even outdoors. If your camera only has an automatic flash, cover the flash's electric eye to fool the camera into thinking it needs to use the flash.

Johnson covered the basics, such as making sure the person in your photo doesn't have a lamp post coming out of his head, and pointed out photographic opportunities that many may have missed. A good picture doesn't have to take in Yosemite's powerful falls or majestic cliffs. It can be as simple as early morning frost on a weed or sunlight refracting through pine branches.

Johnson delved into more advanced photographic lessons, from film speeds to filters. He set up his tripod near the Merced River to photograph the reflection of Half Dome. He then used a polarizer filter, a warming filter, a graduated filter and a special focusing procedure to get the shot he envisioned. The group looked through the lens to see how the filters enhanced the image.

Each camera walk is different, depending on the instructor and the location visited. Participants also get a discount on processing at Yosemite's Photo Center. On certain days, slides taken during that morning's walk are evaluated in an evening slide show—an ideal opportunity for professional feedback.

Another way to bring home creative images of Yosemite is to participate in the Art Activity Center workshops. These free mid-day classes are taught by professional, often well-known, artists in watercolor, etching, drawing and other mediums. Programs are offered from late March through early October. These are for adults and younger students with an earnest interest in art. Classes are held outdoors at inspiring spots, depending on the weather. Bring your own materials or purchase the basics for about $10. Register at the Center.

Junior & Senior Rangers (ages 8-12) are free naturalist activities led by a park ranger. Parents are welcome to accompany their children or drop them off for the day's activities. Kids earn a patch for accomplishing an assigned task. At Happy Isles Nature Center, open 9 to 5 in the summer, the family can check out free daypack kits to help identify birds, rocks and the small delights of the park (tel 209/372-0265 or 209/372-0299).

Yosemite Camera Walk
Yosemite Valley
209/372-1129
Daily, 8:30 A.M.
Free

Notes

A State
for All Seasons

Gloria Ferrer Champagne Caves

Cheers! Will you be toasting in the new year with a bottle of bubbly? There is a good reason why many of us save this tingling libation for special occasions. It takes a minimum of two to four years and eight major steps to transform grapes to champagne.

The Gloria Ferrer Champagne Caves in Sonoma will show you first hand what's behind that glass of sparkling wine. This is one of five wineries run by the Spanish Ferrer family, who have been creating wines for 700 years. Today, the Ferrers are one of the largest producers of sparkling wine in the world.

The first thing the tour guide will tell you is that Gloria Ferrer's product is not champagne at all. Officially, "Champagne" can only be made from grapes grown in the Champagne region of France. Gloria Ferrer produces "sparkling wine" using the methode champenoise.

Methode champenoise means the champagne is created, fermented and sold in the same bottle. Less expensive sparkling wines are fermented in large steel tanks, then transferred to bottles for distribution.

At Gloria Ferrer you learn the basics of champagne-making through their display of antique equipment. The exhibit is strategically placed on a balcony overlooking their state-of-the-art winemaking operation. Although the methode champenoise has evolved into a delicate art enhanced by high technology, it still follows the same basic steps.

Champagne grapes, about 80% Pinot Noir and 20% Chardonnay, are harvested a month before still wine grapes. All are hand-picked and pressed gently. A yeast culture is added and the juice ferments in large steel tanks until the next spring.

The winemaker then creates a unique cuvee, or blend of juices, and adds sugar and yeast for the second fermentation, this time in its own bottle. The bottles are placed, neck tilted down, on riddling racks in Ferrer's subterranean caves.

After 18 months to four years of aging, two workers riddle, or quarter turn, 30,000 bottles a day for a month. More than 50,000 more bottles are riddled by immense machines. Riddling coaxes the yeast sediment to the neck of the bottle. Then the liquid in the neck is frozen and disgorged with the sediment.

Each bottle is topped off with a dosage, or sweetener made with a sugar solution in still wine. The bottle is corked tightly. A wire basket is added to protect the cork from popping under the champagne's pressure. The "punt," or hollow in the bottom of the bottle, also adds strength to protect it from bursting.

Now it's your turn. Champagne used to be reserved for cocktail hour, but now is served throughout a meal and with meat, poultry or fish. It should be consumed within five years after purchase and should always be served chilled.

In selecting champagne, remember that Brut means dry, Dry means sweeter than Brut and Extra Dry is even sweeter. To open champagne, remove the foil and loosen the wire hood. Place a towel over the neck and tilt the bottle slightly. Don't pop the cork. Instead, grasp the bottom of the bottle and pull the bottle out of the cork, not the cork out of the bottle. Enjoy!

Gloria Ferrer Champagne Caves
Highway 121, Sonoma
(5 mi. north of Route 37)
707/996-7256
Tastings 10:30-5:30 daily; Tours on the hour 11-4
Closed major holidays
Samples $2.50-$3.50 per glass
Tours Free

Whale Watching

There's something reassuring about a creature so large and yet so peaceful, who lives in perfect harmony with its own kind and its environment. Perhaps this is why people flock to the coast to see the annual migration of these mighty mammals.

Several spots along the California coast offer excellent vantage points to watch the gray whales and a free and comfortable alternative to whale watching cruises. All you need is the four P's: a warm parka, a picnic lunch, a pair of binoculars and patience.

The peak season for gray whale watching begins in mid-December and January, when the winter cold ices over their Arctic feeding grounds. They head south for warmer waters and shallow, protected lagoons to bear their young.

Pregnant females are the first to head south, usually alone. Courting females and males are next, travelling in groups, or "pods," of three to five. They move at about five miles per hour, covering 70 to 80 miles each day.

Even though gray whales weigh between 20 to 40 tons and are 35 to 50 feet long, they still can be hard to spot. It's best to watch for them with your naked eye. The first sign you'll most likely see is the telltale spout. Once you've spotted the spout, use binoculars for a better view.

Gray whales breathe through a blowhole, actually two nostrils, on top of their heads. When they dive, these nostrils automatically close. The gray whales surface every three to six minutes to breathe, releasing their warm, humid breath as a 10 to 15-foot-high spout. The whale usually spouts three to five times, with more than a minute in between, before diving again.

The gray whale is named for its color. You may see the whale's mottled and barnacle-encrusted back as it arches through the water. Another distinguishing feature is that the gray whale has a low hump on its back rather than a dorsal fin.

If you're lucky, you may see the whale raise its head out of the water to look around. This "spy hopping" is one way the whale can get its bearings. Gray whales also use solar navigation and remember the contours of the ocean bottom.

After spending the summer off the coast of Baja, Mexico, the gray whales head back north to their arctic feeding grounds. You can see them returning along the coast from mid-March through May. This annual migration is one of the longest of any mammal, about 10,000 to 12,000 miles roundtrip.

On the coast north of San Francisco, the Mendocino Coast Botanical Gardens offers a scenic site for whale watching. At Fort Ross State Historic Park, paths lead through a recreation of the old Russian settlement to the rugged coast.

Point Reyes National Seashore is one of the best spots on the coast for whale watching, especially at the Lighthouse. Rangers give talks on gray whales on weekends at 11 and 1.

This area can be crowded, so park at nearby Sir Francis Drake beach and take the free shuttle bus to the lighthouse. You can watch for whales from the upper patio or walk down the 300-plus steps to the lighthouse for a better view (but remember you'll have to climb back up!).

Prime viewing spots south of San Francisco include the Point Montara Lighthouse and Pigeon Point Lighthouse, where whales sometimes come within 50 yards from shore. Near Monterey, Point Lobos State Park also is a prime whale watching point, as well as a stunning natural setting.

Whale Watching
Mendocino Coast Botanical Gardens (see Gardens)
Fort Ross State Historic Park (see Historic Haunts)
Point Reyes Seashore (see The Great Outdoors)
Point Montara (off Hwy. 1, 25 mi. S of SF)
Pigeon Point (off Hwy. 1, Pescadero)
Point Lobos (see The Great Outdoors)
Dec.-Jan. & mid-March-May
Free

Strybing Arboretum

New Zealand may be half-way around the world, but you can see a piece of it right here in San Francisco. The exotic flora of this island nation, and of China, Australia, Japan, Chile and many more are just part of the Strybing Arboretum's "museum of plants."

Located in Golden Gate Park near the de Young Museum, the Strybing offers a compact trip around the world along with insights into the plants that make California unique. It's a delightful sojourn any time of year, especially in spring. It may be the best spot anywhere to celebrate Arbor Day in April.

Maps of the Arboretum are available at the gift shop, but the best way to see this garden is to stroll and discover rather than spend time navigating the maze of winding paths to a particular spot.

The 70-acre Arboretum holds many surprises—the aromatic Garden of Fragrance, the New World Cloud forest, the Mediterranean Cape Province Garden, the Moon-viewing Garden and a dusky grove of towering redwoods to name a few. These are interspersed with spacious lawns, trickling streams and a delightful pond with ducks and a graceful black swan.

It all began in 1937 with a $100,000 bequest from San Francisco flower enthusiast Helen Strybing, along with aid from the city and the federal Works Progress Administration. Today it is home to more than 6,000 species from around the world.

The Garden of Fragrance is a favorite in the Arboretum. You'll know you've found it by the sweet and pungent scents. With plant markings in English and braille, it's enjoyed equally by the visually impaired.

Here you'll find French, Spanish and English lavender, peppermint and lemon balm. One patch is medicinal herbs. Another is culinary herbs including the fragrant winter savory, pineapple sage and French sorrel. The plants are in raised stone beds to entice you to stop and smell the flowers and herbs. You're welcome to feel the texture and press a leaf to release the plant's aromas, but be careful not to damage it.

Nearby is the Biblical Garden, devoted to plants mentioned in the Bible, such as citron and table grape.

The Cape Province Garden represents a Mediterranean climate, with winter rains and summer droughts, the same climate as the Bay Area. Displays explain how plants adapt to the difficult growing weather.

Succulents, like ice plants, store water in their leaves and stems. Their shallow roots quickly absorb large quantities of water from short rains. Annuals, like some daisies, avoid drought by setting seed before drying out. Perennials have succulent leaves or leaves with hair to reflect sunlight.

In the compact California Garden, tour the state's varied habitats, from dry rock garden, to meadow, arroyo, pond and chaparral. Displays explain how plants have adapted to the climate and how man has adapted plants to fit his needs. The exhibit illustrates how Native Americans used Coast Live Oak acorns for food and meadow grass for baskets.

The Redwood Trail is a sharp contrast to the rolling lawns and rock gardens. It is a dark, cool forest of 90-year-old redwoods, giant chain ferns and the clover-leafed redwood sorrel ground cover. In the exotic New World Cloud Forest, plants flourish on the bare branch of a tree.

Allow at least an hour to see the Strybing Arboretum, or, like many visitors, relax for an afternoon on the lawn and benches and enjoy this garden of the world.

Strybing Arboretum
Golden Gate Park, San Francisco
415/661-1514
Open Mon.-Fri. 8-4:30, weekends 10-5
Free

San Bruno Spring Wildflowers

Colorful wildflowers, jungle-like eucalyptus forests, 360-degree panoramas of the San Francisco skyline, Bay and peninsula—this is the surprising San Bruno Mountain Park.

With 2,326 acres, 12 miles of hiking trails and a picnic area nestled in a grassy meadow surrounded by eucalyptus groves, this sanctuary is ideal for an afternoon outing at any time of year. It's particularly delightful from mid-March to mid-May, when the wildflowers are at their peak.

You wouldn't expect to find it here, surrounded by the industrial cities of South San Francisco to the east and Daly City on the west. But this oasis of nature was preserved by the relentless efforts of conservationists and three little butterflies.

The Callippe Silverspot, Mission Blue and San Bruno Elfin are three species of butterflies that call this mountain home. Because they are rare and endangered, their mountain is protected under the federal Endangered Species Act. Each year, a Palo Alto-based firm monitors their progress in an era of ever-encroaching development.

Fourteen species of rare and endangered plant life also are protected by San Bruno Mountain Park, including four rare and endangered manzanitas.

Hikers will appreciate the park's well-planned trails. Several connect to form a variety of loops of differing lengths, terrain and flora. Pick up a brochure/map at the display board at the picnic area parking lot . Choose a route to suit your fancy.

For some of the best wildflowers and views in the Bay Area, try the moderately strenuous, three-mile Summit Trail. The trail begins in sun-dappled woods. The thick, green ivy that blankets the ground and climbs up the tree trunks lends the grove a primeval, rain forest feel.

You then wind along a chapparal-covered hillside. The path is lined with bright yellow goldfields, soft pink flowers and the occasional lacy blue iris. Bright orange California poppies highlight the natural garden. You'll also see clumps of blue-eyed grass and velvety purple violets.

At the crest of the trail, a colorful variety of pink, orange, yellow and purple flowers cover the hillside. Beyond, you can look west over Daly City, then south to the expansive cemeteries of Colma.

Follow the ridgeline towards the radio towers. A short but steep climb brings you to the summit. You are following in the footsteps of the early Spanish explorers, who climbed San Bruno Mountain to reconnoiter the surrounding land and water.

You get a tremendous view of the Bay Area on a clear day. Be aware, however, that San Bruno Mountain is a micro-climate of its environs, complete with fog and high winds. Be sure to bring a jacket for the ridge walk, and don't be surprised if a haze obscures your view of the city.

Wildflower gardens bloom on the hillside as you head back down. Here you can sidetrack on the Dairy Ravine trail to the Eucalyptus Loop Trail, which borders a dense jungle of eucalyptus forest. Follow the trail either way to circle back to your starting point.

If you prefer not to hike, you also can drive to the radio towers on the summit and take a short walk along the ridge for the views and wildflowers.

San Bruno Mountain Park
555 Guadalupe Canyon Parkway, Brisbane
415/992-6770
Open daily 8-Sunset
$3 per vehicle on weekends and holidays

Sonoma's Summer Harvest

If you like apples and berries, you'll love the stretch from Sebastopol to the Russian River in summertime. You can indulge in delicious produce fresh from the tree and vine, much of it organically grown. You can sip wine at the area's diverse vineyards. You can even take a dip in the Russian River if it gets too hot.

Best of all, you can stop by Kozlowski farms for a free taste of their mouth-watering jams, salsas, chutneys, mustards, dessert sauces and more.

Gravenstein apples grow in abundance here, so much so that they've named Route 116 the "Gravenstein Highway." Orchards border this country road, their branches heavy with ripe apples in season. In mid-August a fair celebrates this robust fruit.

You'll also see Christmas tree farms, miniature forests that give hours of delight to families during the holidays. Many invite visitors to choose and cut their own tree for an old-fashioned family outing.

Many cottage industries live off the land in this area. You can stop by and see their businesses first hand. Me Gusta Farm in Sebastopol specializes in French-style goat cheese and no-spray salad greens (965 Martin Ln., Sebastopol, tel. 707/823-1322, Open Mar.-Nov., Mon.-Sat., call for hours).

Hallsberg's Apple Farm offers 48 varieties of apples during picking season from late summer to early fall. You pick the best of each harvest from bins. (2500 Gravenstein Hwy, Sebastopol, tel. 707/829-0187, Open Aug 1-Nov. 15, Daily 10-6)

As you near the town of Forestville, be sure to stop by Kozlowski Farms at 5566 Gravenstein Highway, on the left hand side of the road. In their open-air store, you can try almost all of their bountiful line of well over 50 gourmet products.

Jars open for sampling on the day you visit may include three kinds of mustard like Ol' Uncle Cal's Sweet-n-Hot and a dozen jams from Blackberry to Golden Raspberry to Kiwi. You can indulge in several dessert sauces like the irresistible Raspberry Fudge, or try Peach Chutney, Red Raspberry Vinegar, Chunky Apple Sauce and many more.

The farm is truly a family-run operation. Tony and Carmen Kozlowski began farming here in 1947. In 1968, following a bumper crop of apples, they planted 15 acres of red raspberries. Soon, Carmen began making jam in her kitchen. Today, the whole family helps out , from the farming to the marketing.

Kozlowski products have been written up in Gourmet magazine and caught the attention of Julia Child, who filmed segments of Good Morning America here. Best of all, they sell at this farm stand at an average $4 a jar, about one dollar less than upscale department stores and supermarkets.

During the late summer, you also can buy fresh raspberries, blackberries, golden raspberries and apples here. Their cider is known as some of the best around. Enjoy all of these with your picnic lunch at the tables overlooking the rolling hills.

To top off the day, take a left on River Road to Korbel Champagne Cellars. This is a grand, ivy-covered building with colorful, inviting gardens. Tasting and cellars tours are offered year-round. In summer, you're invited to join special garden tours. (13250 River Rd., Guerneville, tel. 707/887-2294, Open daily 9-5:30 in summer, 9-5 in winter.)

Before heading to this bountiful area, send a self-addressed, stamped envelope to the address below to receive a free Sonoma County Farm Trails map. This colorful brochure is packed with information. It tells which produce is available by month, describes its nearly 150 members and lists special events.

Sonoma County Farm Trails
P.O. Box 6032
707/586-3276
Free

Delta Drive

The Sacramento River delta is ideal for an old-fashioned Sunday drive, especially on a warm summer afternoon. Fishermen, houseboaters, waterskiers and windsurfers are all out to enjoy the cool waters of this slow-poke river.

If you've only got a day to get away from it all, this scenic loop winds along the river, takes in two old-fashioned ferry rides and stops at historic small towns. It begins as you cross the bridge from Antioch on Route 160 into Delta country.

This is Sherman Island. It doesn't look like much today—a flat, green expanse—but it looked like even less in the past. Like other islands that make up Delta Country, this was once mosquito-infested swampland. The first Spanish explorers passed it off as a treacherous everglade.

About 30,000 Native Americans called it home, enjoying the bounty of edible wild plants, tule elk, beaver, salmon and waterfowl. Then came the trappers. From 1830 to 1845 they commandeered the area, selling beaver, otter and mink pelts to the Hudson Bay Company. By the 1840s, farmers also recognized the potential of the Delta's rich soil.

In 1848, the sleepy delta was thrust awake by cries of Gold! Paddlewheel steamers were some of the more than 250 delta vessels that ferried fortune-seekers to the Mother Lode. Before long, the less jubilant miners returned. Some settled on the delta to farm. The formation of levees, islands and arable farmland, a process called reclamation, began.

If you plan to camp or picnic on the Delta, stop by Brannan Island State Recreation Area. This preserve offers shaded tent sites, group picnic areas, tables and barbecues near the river, and a small beach with calm water for swimming.

At the next bridge, take a left onto Route 12 and follow the signs to Rio Vista. Foster's Big Horn Saloon, at 143 Main Street, is the most intriguing spot in town. Great White Hunter William Foster collected more than 300 animal trophies from around the world at a time when it was considered a fashionable adventure. On the walls you'll see lions, antelope, an African elephant and more, as well as pictures showing Foster in the field with his kills.

For a touch or modern-day nostalgia, stroll to the waterfront to see a marble monument dedicated to none other than wayward Humphrey the Humpback Whale, who played in the waters here in 1985.

Backtrack out of town, then follow the signs to Ryer Island and our first ferry ride on the diesel-powered "Real McCoy." It's small, transporting just a few cars at a time across to the island. Like all Delta ferries, it is free and runs continuously, with short breaks at lunch and dinner. At one time, ferries were the only way to "island hop" in the Delta. Now, drawbridges have replaced all but a few.

Take a right off the Real McCoy and circle the outer edge of Ryer Island to the Grand Island ferry. This vessel pulls itself along a cable strung across the water. When not in use, the cable rests on the bottom so boats can pass. Take a left off the ferry, along the shore of Grand Island to the graceful Grand Island Mansion on the right. This stately, plantation-style home with the cypress-lined circular drive was built in 1917.

From Grand Island, follow the signs across the drawbridge to Locke. This ancient-looking town was founded in 1915, the only rural town in the U.S. to be built entirely by Chinese. Explore the street below the levee road, with its rickety wooden buildings and old Chinese markings. For more on Locke, see "Towns to Explore," pages 112-113.

As a last stop, art deco lovers should cross back over the river to Grand Island and visit the pink-colored Grand Island Inn where you can relax with a soda in prohibition-era surroundings and watch the slow-poke Delta waters flow by.

California Delta Chambers
49 Main St., Box 177, Isleton, CA 95641
916/777-5007

Monarch Butterflies

It's like walking into a storybook. Bright orange and black Monarch butterflies—thousands of them—flutter like a kaleidoscope around you, cling to the sweet-smelling eucalyptus and prance on tangled berry bushes.

This is Natural Bridges State Park in Santa Cruz, winter home to the Monarch, the queen of butterflies. Just how many of these regal winged creatures will visit in an average year? One thousand? Ten thousand? Keep counting. Each year, as many as 160,000 Monarch butterflies spend the colder months in this compact eucalyptus grove. They begin to appear in mid-October and leave again in February.

A raised wooden walkway brings you down the hill, into the forest and to a patio in the midst of butterfly country. The best time to come is mid-day, when the warm sun beams into the shady canyon and the butterflies are most active. Monarchs can't fly at temperatures lower than 55 degrees and are unable to move at all when the mercury sinks below 40 degrees.

The Monarchs come from as far away as Idaho, Colorado, Montana and British Columbia, wending their way over mountains, cities, fields and lakes. Even more remarkable is that these are not the same Monarchs that stayed here last winter. Three to five generational cycles—mating, laying eggs, the new caterpillar transforming to an adult butterfly, the parent butterfly's death—have passed. Yet the great, great grandchildren of those who wintered in Santa Cruz know to head for the coast and warmer climes when the days start getting shorter. How do they find their way?

"The navigation aspects of Monarch biology are the most intriguing and least understood," said John

Lane, a Santa Cruz biologist who has been studying butterflies for 30 years and Monarchs in particular for twelve. Some believe that Monarchs have an inborn sun compass, which directs them according to the position of the sun. They are also tuned in to the Earth's magnetic pole. Lane compares their double-edged navigational systems to "a high-quality jetliner."

Many of the Monarchs you see in this grove will be hanging in clusters from the drooping eucalyptus branches. At first, with their folded wings, they appear almost like leaves, layered one on top of the other similar to shingles on a roof. This is a form of group protection. They not only stay warmer, but the rain slides off more easily and the weight of the many butterflies prevents the branch from swaying in the wind.

In spring they start a new year of migration. The Monarchs mate while migrating and egg-laden females must fly in search of milkweed plants to deposit their eggs. Some head north; others south to New Mexico and Arizona. Generations of monarchs continue to migrate and spread their population to the north and east until autumn urges the butterflies to return.

Inside the visitor center, informative displays tell the story of the Monarch and migration. You can touch a delicate butterfly wing or feel the soft fur of an otter in the exhibit focusing on the park's other natural highlights.

There's more to do at Natural Bridges than visit butterflies. Take a walk along the beach to the rock arch that gave the park its name. Have a picnic. Build a sand castle. Or explore the mussels and anemones in the tidal pools at low tide. Like the Monarchs, you, too, can enjoy a cool weather day in the seashore town of Santa Cruz.

Natural Bridges State Park
West Cliff Dr., Santa Cruz
Open daily 8 A.M.-sunset
408/423-4609
$6 per car, includes same-day admission
to other state parks and beaches

Salmon Run
Taylor Creek

What's at the end of the Rainbow Trail? Follow the winding path through shimmering aspens, over trickling streams, around a grassy meadow and you will find a fisherman's dream—an underwater view of a pool full of brown, rainbow and brook trout.

The pool is especially colorful in October, when Kokanee Salmon, which are dwarf, land-locked sockeye salmon, spawn here. These fascinating fish have blue backs and silvery sides except in mating, when both sexes turn a brilliant red and males develop hooked jaws and humped backs. The salmon return to spawn in the stream of their births, lay eggs, and die.

These are just some of the intriguing facts you'll find on the displays along the trail at the Forest Service Taylor Creek Area near South Lake Tahoe. Nearby, the Trail of the Washoe offers a glimpse into life at Tahoe before the white man. The trail to Tallac Historic Site circles turn-of-the-century mansions. The Visitor Center, where the trails begin, is just north of Camp Richardson along Route 89.

Children and adults enjoy the short, level Rainbow Trail to the Stream Profile Chamber. Markers along the way point out the natural diversity of this compact area. The trail starts out through dry, sparse land, then slopes downward through a small aspen grove, then winds through a wet meadow. You can conduct experiments, such as measuring the water flow of a stream with a gallon can, to better understand the importance of water here.

The most popular stop along the Trail is the underground viewing chamber. A wall of windows reveals the Rainbow Pool and its fishy residents. In addition to the salmon displays, others illustrate how fish see two things at once and how their scales can be used like tree rings to determine age. Small aquariums contain crawdads, tadpoles and minnows.

On the self-guiding Trail of the Washoe, you learn that Native Americans turned sage bush into coarse material for beds, seating mats and diapers. buck brush thorns were used for tatooing. They ate manzanita berries and used branches for snowshoes.

Markers along the Trail describe how they lived and worked with the land. In one piece of bedrock are six-inch deep holes, or mortars, worn smooth by centuries of use. You can grind seeds into flour in these holes using crude stone pestles.

You can either hike or drive to the Tallac Historic Site. These sprawling estates were built around the turn of the century as summer homes for wealthy San Franciscans.

The 1894 Pope House was purchased by George Pope in 1923. This mansion has four bedrooms, four baths, 13 closets, two fireplaces, an entry hall and a butlers pantry. That's just the beginning.

The estate's buildings include a dairy, ice house, laundry and kitchen. The family and guests played on polo fields and tennis courts nearby. An idyllic, wooded garden with an arched footbridge and rock waterfall is reminiscent of a Monet painting.

Other nearby mansions include the 1920 Baldwin-McGonagle estate and the 1923 Valhalla, built by San Francisco broker, Walter Heller.

Even if you can't come during the salmon spawning season, Taylor Creek is worth a visit at any time of year. Although the underground viewing chamber is closed in the colder months, the trails are ideal for hiking and cross-country skiing.

Forest Service Taylor Creek Area
Route 89 near South Lake Tahoe
(1/2-mi. north of Camp Richardson)
916/573-2674
Stream Profile Chamber and Visitor Center
open daily 8-5:30 Memorial Day-Labor Day;
Sat. & Sun. 9-4 in October
Free

Where It's At

These spotting maps and brief descriptions of the 101 excursions will help you plan your afternoon, daytrip or weekend getaway. You may want to see more than one excursion in an area or add a new side trip to an old favorite destination. There's plenty to see, do and learn. Remember, it's all affordable!

Symbols Used

 Behind the Scenes

 For Kids of All Ages

 We Got Culture

 Towns to Explore

 Literary Landmarks

 Gardens

 Historic Haunts

 The Great Outdoors

A State for All Seasons

R   Restrooms
F   Food sold on premises
P   Free parking in vicinity

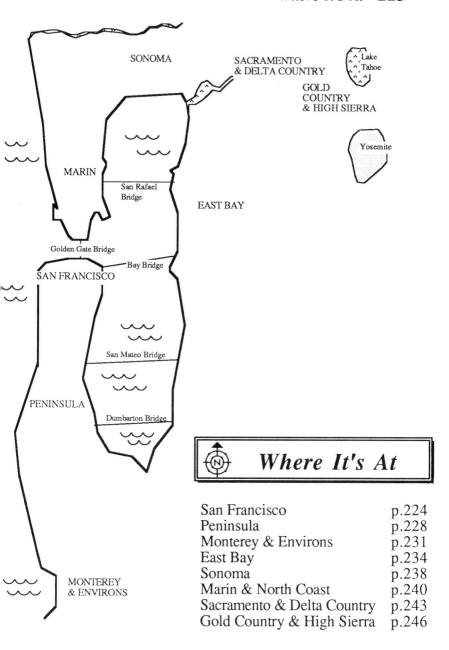

SONOMA

SACRAMENTO
& DELTA COUNTRY

Lake
Tahoe

GOLD
COUNTRY
& HIGH SIERRA

Yosemite

MARIN

San Rafael
Bridge

EAST BAY

Golden Gate Bridge

Bay Bridge

SAN FRANCISCO

San Mateo Bridge

PENINSULA

Dumbarton Bridge

Where It's At

MONTEREY
& ENVIRONS

San Francisco

A S	Academy of Sciences
A	Alcatraz
A A	Asian Art Museum
CC	Cable Car Barn Museum
C	Chinese Historical Society
CT	Coit Tower
D	de Young Museum
F	Fort Mason Ethnic Museums
HL	Haas-Lilienthal House
H	Hyde Street Pier
J	Japanese Tea and The Conservatory
L	Levi Strauss Factory
M	Mission San Francisco de Asis
MM	Musée Mécanique
N	North Beach
O	Old Mint & Ansel Adams Center
S	Strybing Arboretum
W	Walking Tours

SAN FRANCISCO

Academy of Sciences. Journey back in time, to outer space and to the depths of the ocean in this fun museum. **R F P** - **28**

Alcatraz. The prison within the prison system. Legendary inmates include Al Capone, Machine Gun Kelly and Robert "The Birdman" Stroud. **R** - **152**

Asian Art Museum. The world's largest collection of Asian Art outside Asia. Cost includes same-day admission to the de Young Museum next door. **R F P** - **62**

Cable Car Barn Museum. See the inner workings of our nation's only moving National Historic Landmark. **R** - **30**

Chinese Historical Society. The story of San Francisco's Chinese heritage, just a few blocks from Chinatown. - **64**

Coit Tower. Recently refurbished social realist murals, painted in the 1930s. Ride the elevator to the top of the tower for one of the city's best views. **R P** - **66**

de Young Museum. A journey through American culture through art. Free docent tours. Museum price includes same-day admission to the Asian Art Museum next door. **R F P** - **68**

SAN FRANCISCO (continued)

☼ *Fort Mason Ethnic Museums.*
Museums devoted to folk and contemporary art from
America, Africa, Italy & Mexico. Gift shops with
fun folk art for sale. **R F** (vegetarian) **P**   **- 70**

☼ *Haas-Lilienthal House.* Step back to
the Victorian era during a tour of this 1886 home.
Many original furnishings. **R P**   **- 72**

🚂 *Hyde Street Pier.* Welcome aboard
this fine collection of historic ships, located right
across from The Cannery. **R**   **- 32**

🌸 *Japanese Tea & The Conservatory.*
Stroll past a bonsai forest, 200-year-old Buddha,
carp ponds and pagodas. See orchids and tropical
plants in The Conservatory, a Victorian-era "crystal
palace" greenhouse. **R F** (tea & cookies) **P** **- 136**

👁 *Levi Strauss.* A behind-the-scenes look at
how the original 501 blue jean is stitched together.
Film. Small museum with antique Levi's. **R**   **- 4**

🐻 *Mission San Francisco de Asis.*
The oldest intact building in San Francisco.
Restored 1791 mission established by Father
Junipero Serra **R P**   **- 154**

SAN FRANCISCO (continued)

Musée Mécanique. One of the world's largest private collections of antique amusements, located at the Cliff House. **R F P** - **34**

North Beach. Taste a slice of Italy and learn about the area's Italian heritage in North Beach. Walking tour and museum. **F P** **- 74**

Old Mint & Ansel Adams Center. See the Old Mint's $4 million in gold and create a commemorative medal. Vintage photographs and contemporary works displayed at the Ansel Adams Center. **R** **- 76**

Strybing Arboretum. Celebrate spring at this "museum of plants" and its collection of flora from around the world. **R P** **- 210**

Walking Tours. See San Francisco's hidden history on these free City Guides tours. Eighteen tours offered year-round. **- 6**

Peninsula

A	Acres of Orchids
B	Barbie Doll Hall of Fame
G	The Garage
H	Hakone Gardens & Cultural Center
HM	Half Moon Bay
R	Rodin Sculpture Garden
RM	Rosicrucian Egyptian Museum
W	San Bruno Spring Wildflowers
SJ	San Jose Historical Park
S	Saso Herb Gardens
SM	Sunset Magazine

PENINSULA

👁 *Acres of Orchids.* See how these beautiful plants are grown from the world's tiniest seed. A greenhouse tour of the world's largest orchid hybridizer. Retail shop. **R P** - **8**

🚂 *Barbie Doll Hall of Fame.* Over 16,000 Barbies, clothes & accessories packed into this compact museum in Palo Alto. **R P** - **36**

🚂 *The Garage.* Learn how computers work. Fun hands-on exhibits. **R F** - **38**

🌸 *Hakone Gardens.* A tranquil oasis of old Japan, punctuated with traditional Japanese homes. **R F**(tea & sweets) **P**(free weekdays) - **138**

☁ *Half Moon Bay.* Gardens, boutiques, beaches, a winery and more. Annual pumpkin and Chamarita festivals. **R F P** - **96**

☀ *Rodin Sculpture Garden.* Selection of masterpieces from world's 2nd largest collection of Rodin. Includes Gates of Hell. - **78**

☀ *Rosicrucian Egyptian Museum.* Artifacts from ancient Egypt, including life-size tomb, mummies, stone tablets. **R P** - **80**

🦋 *San Bruno Spring Wildflowers.* Views & blooms south of San Francisco. **R P** - **212**

PENINSULA (continued)

 San Jose Historical Park. 100-year-old buildings, village setting. **R F**(ice cream) **P - 156**

 Saso Herb Gardens. Family-run herb garden. Tours. Retail shop. **P**   **- 140**

 Sunset Magazine. Tour offices & gardens of the Magazine of Western Living. **R P**   **- 10**

Symbols Used

	Behind the Scenes
	For Kids of All Ages
	We Got Culture
	Towns to Explore
	Literary Landmarks
	Gardens
	Historic Haunts
	The Great Outdoors
	A State for All Seasons
R	**Restrooms**
F	**Food sold on premises**
P	**Free parking in vicinity**

Monterey & Environs

C	Carmel Mission
G	Gilroy & Environs
L	Long Marine Laboratory
MB	Monarch Butterflies
M	Monterey
MS	Mystery Spot
P	Pinnacles National Monument
PL	Point Lobos State Reserve
R	Robinson Jeffers' Tor House
W	Wilder Ranch State Park

MONTEREY & ENVIRONS

Carmel Mission. Restored 200-year-old mission, California's first library, Father Junipero Serra's tomb. **R P**   **- 158**

Gilroy & Environs. Driving tour to wineries, outlet stores, San Juan Bautista Historic Park and Mission. **R F P**   **- 98**

Long Marine Laboratory. A behind-the-scenes look at a school for sea lions. Blue whale skeleton. Aquarium with touch tank. **R P**   **- 12**

Monarch Butterflies.. See 160,000 butterflies in one compact eucalyptus grove. Peak season is October through February. **R**   **- 218**

Monterey. Walking tour on Monterey's Path of History. Custom House, California's first theater, 19th-century general store, site where California's first constitution written. **R F**   **- 100**

The Mystery Spot. See a golf ball roll uphill and people shrink and grow in this fun, mysterious site near Santa Cruz. **R P**   **- 40**

Pinnacles National Monument. Hike below, around and above odd rock spires. Explore dark caves with a flashlight. Watch rock climbers. See tarantulas and wild pigs. **R**   **- 196**

MONTEREY & ENVIRONS (continued)

Point Lobos State Reserve. Called the "greatest meeting of land and water in the world." Rugged coastline, small historic museum, sea lion rocks, tide pools. **R**   **- 198**

Robinson Jeffers' Tor House. An oasis of old Carmel at this poet's residence. Romantic Hawk Tower built of stone by Jeffers. Guided tours enhanced by Jeffers' poems. **P - 122**

Wilder Ranch State Park. Restored turn-of-the-century dairy farm. Costumed docents perform traditional chores on weekends. Two miles north of Santa Cruz. **R**   **- 160**

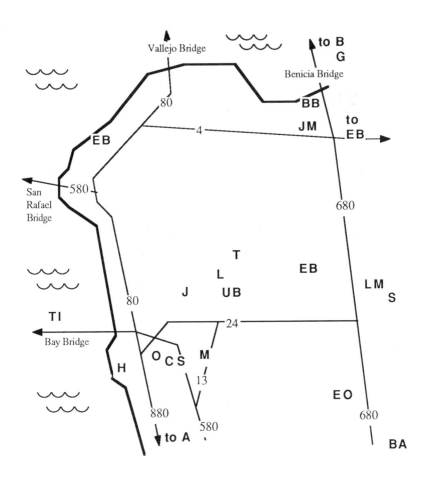

East Bay

A	Ardenwood Historic Farm	**J**	Judah L. Magnes Museum
B A	Behring Auto Museum	**L**	Lawrence Hall of Science
B	Benicia	**LM**	Lindsay Museum
B B	Bocce, Biking, Birdwatching	**M**	Mormon Temple
C S	Camron-Stanford House	**O**	Oakland Museum
E B	East Bay Parks	**S**	Shadelands Ranch
EO	Eugene O'Neill's Tao House	**T**	Tilden Regional Park
G	Glass Blowers of Benicia	**TI**	Treasure Island
H	Heinhold's Saloon	**U B**	UC Berkeley Botanical Garden
JM	John Muir Historic Site		

EAST BAY

Ardenwood Historic Farm. Relive history on a Victorian-era farm. Harvest crops with traditional hand tools. Ride a horse-powered railroad or wagon. Visit farm animals. Watch a blacksmith at work. **R F P**   **- 162**

Behring Auto Museum. One of the world's best collections of classic automobiles. One-of-a-kind sports cars, autos owned by Hollywood celebrities and royalty. **R P**   **- 82**

Benicia. Walking tour, including one of California's first state capitol buildings, 19th-century hotel, fun shops, historic buildings. **R F P - 102**

Bocce, Biking and Birdwatching Official bocce courts, Joe DiMaggio ball field, salt water marsh, bike trails and more along Martinez waterfront. **R P**   **- 42**

Camron-Stanford House.   Guided tours of restored, furnished 1876 Victorian mansion. Exhibit room on restoration process.   **- 164**

East Bay Parks. Includes Black Diamond Mines in Antioch, Briones in central Contra Costa County and Point Pinole along San Pablo Bay. **R**(outhouses) **P**(free at Black Diamond)   **- 186**

EAST BAY (continued)

Eugene O'Neill's Tao House.
Home where playwright lived and wrote "The Iceman Cometh, "Hughie," "Moon for the Misbegotten" and more. **P** - **124**

Glass Blowers of Benicia. See molten glass transformed into delicate vases, perfume bottles and stemware. **P** - **14**

Heinhold's First and Last Chance Saloon. Jack London studied here as a child and overheard sea-faring tales recounted later in his books. Historic photos, memorabilia. **R** - **126**

John Muir Historic Site. Muir's Victorian home and fruit ranch. Writings on conservation from his "scribble den" here initiated preservation of many national parks. **R P** - **128**

Judah L. Magnes Museum. Third largest Jewish museum in the United States. Exhibits on the Sabbath, Jewish history, holidays. Judaica library. **R P** (limited, on street) - **84**

Lawrence Hall of Science. Fun hands-on exhibits on holography, lasers and eyesight. Walk-in model of brain. Weekend workshops, star-gazing. **R F P** - **44**

EAST BAY (continued)

Lindsay Museum. Learn more about the wild creatures in our own backyard. Permanent family with bobcat, opossum, raccoon and owls. Visitor-animal interaction. **R P**   **- 46**

Mormon Temple. Guided tours of grounds and Inter-Stake center at this landmark temple high in the Oakland hills. Introduction to Mormon religion. Genealogical library. **R P   - 86**

Oakland Museum. Three floors of superb exhibits focusing on California's natural history, heritage, culture and art.. **R F   - 48**

Shadelands Ranch. 1903 Colonial Revival home, with original furnishings, reflects farm life of early 20th century. **R P   - 166**

Tilden Regional Park. Fun for the whole family. Wilderness trails. Miniature steam train. Little Farm with pigs, sheep. Botanic Garden. Antique carousel. **R**(Lake Anza, Merry-go-round) **P   - 50**

Treasure Island. Former site of the 1939 Golden Gate International Exposition. Now a military base. Museum with military and exposition memorabilia. View of San Francisco. **R P   - 168**

UC Berkeley Botanical Garden. Encompasses more than 12,000 species and varieties of plants from around the world. California natives, tropicals, Oriental medicinal herbs. **R P   - 142**

Sonoma

C	California Cooperative Creamery
G F	Gloria Ferrer Champagne Caves
L	Jack London State Historic Park
L B	Luther Burbank & Kyoto Koi
P	Petaluma Adobe
S S	Snoopy & Skating
S	Sonoma
S S H	Sonoma's Summer Harvest
Y	YaKaAma & California Carnivores

SONOMA

California Cooperative Creamery.
See how milk becomes cheese. Extensive selection
of gifts with dairy cow motif. **R F P** **- 16**

*Gloria Ferrer Champagne
Caves.* See how sparkling wine is made. Tips on
selecting and serving champagne. **R P** **- 206**

Jack London State Historic Park.
Eerie ruins of Wolf House. London's study,
memorabilia. 800-acre park. Picnic area. **R - 130**

Luther Burbank & Kyoto Koi.
Garden monument to famous botanist. Retail
nursery with bonsai garden, koi. **R P** **- 144**

Petaluma Adobe. Restored, furnished
1830s Mexican rancho. Farm animals. **R P - 170**

Snoopy & Skating. Original Peanuts
cartoons, memorabilia. World's largest collection of
Peanuts gifts. Ice arena. **R F P** **- 52**

Sonoma. Walking tour of Plaza. Historic
buildings, mission, fun shops. **R F P** **- 104**

Sonoma's Summer Harvest. Apples,
berries, free tastes of jams, sauces. **R F P** **- 214**

YaKaAma & California Carnivores.
Native American and insect-eating plants. Retail
plant sales at both. **R P** **- 146**

Marin & North Coast

CC	China Camp State Park
FR	Fort Ross State Historic Park
MC	Marin County Civic Center
MH	Marin Headlands
M	Mendocino
MB	Mendocino Botanical Gardens
MW	Muir Woods National Monument
O	Oldest Working Oyster Farm
P	Point Reyes National Seashore
R	Richardson Bay Audubon Center
S A	San Anselmo
S	Sausalito
WW	Whale Watching

MARIN & NORTH COAST

🐻 *China Camp State Park.* Last remnant of Chinese fishing villages that once dotted coast of San Pablo Bay. Small museum. Picnic grounds with water views. Hiking. Birdwatching. **R F** (snack bar open on busy weekends) **P** - **172**

🐻 *Fort Ross State Historic Park.* Restored wooden fort. One of Russia's early pioneer outposts. Visitor Center. **R** - **174**

☀️ *Marin County Civic Center.* Guided tours of Frank Lloyd Wright's sculpture of a building. **R F P** - **88**

🌲*Marin Headlands.* Explore hiking trails, World War II batteries, lighthouse, beaches. Excellent views of Golden Gate Bridge and San Francisco. **R**(outhouses) **P** - **188**

👣*Mendocino.* Walking tour of historic side of Mendocino. Museum. Victorians. Kuan Ti Temple. "Murder, She Wrote" house. **R F P** - **110**

🌷 *Mendocino Coast Botanical Gardens..* More than 3,000 varieties of native and cultivated plants in over 20 plant communities. Hidden pioneer cemetery. Superb views of Pacific. Whale watching in season. **R P** - **148**

MARIN & NORTH COAST (continued)

Muir Woods National Monument. Walk among the world's tallest living things. Redwoods, wildflowers, deer. **R F P** **- 190**

Oldest Working Oyster Farm. Weatherworn buildings in quiet setting belie nearly 2 million oysters in water. Buy oysters to eat. **R**(outhouses) **F**(oysters) **P** **- 18**

Point Reyes National Seashore. Earthquake Trail along San Andreas Fault. Wilderness hikes to secluded beaches. Miwok Indian Village. Historic Lighthouse. **R P** **- 192**

Richardson Bay Audubon Center. A 900-acre sanctuary, just outside of Tiburon. 1876 restored Victorian. Nature trail. Peak bird migration is October through April. **P** **- 194**

San Anselmo. More than 130 antique dealers within half a mile. **R F P** **- 106**

Sausalito. A sunny getaway just north of Golden Gate Bridge. Walking tour explores back roads and historic sites of town. **R F** **- 108**

Whale Watching. The best coastal sites to watch for whales. Tips on how to locate whales and why they migrate. Peak season is mid-December through January and mid-March through May. **R P**(depending on site) **- 208**

Sacramento & Delta Country

A	Anheuser Busch Beer Brewery
B	Blue Diamond Almond Factory
C	Crocker Art Museum
D	Delta Drive
J	Jelly Belly Factory
L	Locke
O	Old Sacramento
RR	California State Railroad Museum
S	Sutter's Fort
TF	Towe Ford Museum
T	Travis Air Force Museum
WR	Western Railway Museum

SACRAMENTO & DELTA COUNTRY

👁 *Anheuser Busch Beer Brewery.*
See how the King of Beers is aged, bottled and packaged in the world's largest brewery. **R P** - **20**

👁 *Blue Diamond Almond Factory.*
Watch almonds being blanched, sorted, quality-checked and packaged in the world's largest almond processing plant. **R** F(almonds) **P** - **24**

☼ *Crocker Art Museum.* Oldest public art museum in the west, housed in a magnificent 1871 mansion. Works by California and European masters. **R P** - **90**

🦋 *Delta Drive.* An old-fashioned driving tour for a sunny summer afternoon. Free ferry boat rides, houseboats, art deco hotel. **R F P** - **216**

👁 *Jelly Belly Factory.* Watch jelly belly jelly beans being created. Free samples on tour. Candy gift shop. **R** F(candy) **P** - **22**

👣 *Locke.* Only rural town in U.S. built entirely by Chinese. Gambling house museum. Weathered buildings. Import shops. **R F P** - **112**

SACRAMENTO
& DELTA COUNTRY (continued)

Old Sacramento. Five fun history museums. See $1 million in gold. Send a telegraph to a friend. Visit 1870s railroad depot. **R F** - **114**

California State Railroad Museum. Explore above, on board and below 21 beautifully restored locomotives and railroad cars. One of the finest museums of its kind. **R** - **54**

Sutter's Fort. Restored, furnished 1846 fort. One of first settlements in California. Exhibit rooms. Sound wand narrates history. **R** - **176**

Towe Ford Museum. World's most complete collection of antique Fords. More than 170 cars on display. Near Old Sacramento. **R P** - **92**

Travis Air Force Museum. More than 20 aircraft on display, including helicopters, immense transport planes, bombers and jets. Air Force and NASA exhibits. **R P** - **56**

Western Railway Museum. Ride on an antique trolley car. See antique passenger cars, cabooses, unusual railroad cars. **R P** - **58**

Gold Country
& High Sierra

C	Columbia State Historic Park
D	Donner Memorial State Park
MT	Mark Twain in Gold Country
M	Mariposa Grove of Big Trees
YP	Pioneer Yosemite History Center
TC	Salmon Run, Taylor Creek
T	Truckee
V	Volcano
Y	Yosemite Camera Walk

GOLD COUNTRY & HIGH SIERRA

Columbia State Historic Park. A living history town from the gold rush era. Ride a stage. Pan for gold. **R F P** - **178**

Donner Memorial State Park. Learn the history of our nation's most tragic pioneer story at the site where it all happened. **R P** - **180**

Mark Twain in Gold Country. See where Twain heard and wrote Jumping Frog story. **R F**(in Angels Camp, Murphy's) **P** - **132**

Mariposa Grove of Big Trees. Walk among world's largest living things. **R P** - **200**

Pioneer Yosemite History Center. Century-old buildings in village setting. Costumed docents in summer. **P** - **182**

Salmon Run, Taylor Creek. Nature trails. Underwater view of pond with trout, salmon. Peak salmon run is Oct. **R F P** - **220**

Truckee. History of railroad town. Fun shops. **R F P** - **116**

Volcano. The gold country town that tourism forgot. **R F P** - **118**

Yosemite Camera Walk. Free camera walks, art workshops, more. **R F P** - **202**

```
┌─────────────────────────────────┐
│                                 │
│          Bonus                  │
│          Coupon                 │
│          Section                │
│                                 │
└─────────────────────────────────┘
```

Bonus Coupon Section

Save with these bonus coupons to some of the area's most popular attractions!

* Described in this guide. See Table of Contents.

California Academy of Sciences

$1.00 off for Youths, 17 and under

One of the largest natural history museums in the world, including Steinhart Aquarium and Morrison Planetarium.

❧ CROCKER ART MUSEUM ❧
ONE FREE ADMISSION WITH ONE PAID ADMISSION

Experience the Crocker Art Museum - spectacular Victorian architecture, Early California paintings, and colorful contemporary California art.

Good through Dec. 31, 1993   (916) 449-5423

EXPLORATORIUM
3601 Lyon Street
San Francisco
California 94123

$1.00 off
Adult Admission

Maximum 4 per coupon.   Not good with other discount offers.

California Academy of Sciences

Open 10 AM-5 PM every day.
Open July 4-Labor Day 10 AM-7 PM

Music Concourse, Golden Gate Park, San Francisco, CA 94118-4599.
For more information, call 415/750-7145.

3rd & 'O' Streets ❦ Sacramento, CA 95814

❦ Open Wednesday - Sunday, 10 am - 5 pm ❦
Thursday evening until 9 pm

Closed Monday, Tuesday, and major holidays

(916) 449-5423

Exploratorium

America's #1 hands-on museum of science, art, and human perception with over 650 interactive exhibits to touch, play, hear, look--to delight in. Fun for all ages.
Tu.-Sun. 10 AM-5 PM; Wed. 10 AM-9:30 PM.
Located in the Palace of Fine Arts, close to the Golden Gate Bridge and opposite the San Francisco Marina.
Travel directions 415/561-0399.
Recorded information 415/561-0360.

$1.00 off Regular Adult Admission
50¢ off Regular Child Admission

Maximum 6 per coupon. Not good with other discount offers. Expires 12/31/93.

HYDE STREET PIER

$1.00 off regular adult admission

Regular admission: $3 Adults (ages 17-61); Seniors and Children (16 and under) are Free. Expires 12/31/93.

USS PAMPANITO

World War II Fleet Submarine

$1.00 off regular adult admission

Regular admission: $4 Adults; $2 Jrs (ages 12-17); $1 Seniors and Children (ages 6-12). Expires 12/31/93.

the Guinness Museum of World Records

See record-breaking exhibits of the world's TALLEST & **BIGGEST**, LARGEST & smallest. Re-creations, 3-D demonstrations & videos of records being set! Sun.-Thurs. 10 AM-10PM; Fri./Sat. 10AM-Midnight. At Fisherman's Wharf between Taylor & Jones on Jefferson St. Across from the fishing fleet. Call 415/202-9852.

Hyde Street Pier

Operated by the National Park Service. Home to three historic vessels: the square rigger BALCLUTHA, the lumber schooner CA THAYER and the ferry boat EUREKA. Explore meticulously restored cabins and examine detailed displays. Watch riggers working high aloft and shipwrights using traditional skills. Located at the foot of Hyde St. at Jefferson St. Call 415/556-3002.

USS PAMPANITO

Operated by the National Maritime Museum Association. A World War II balao class submarine located at Pier 45 near Fisherman's Wharf. Tour its cramped living quarters and view its arsenal of ten torpedo tubes and a 5-inch deck gun. An audio tour describing the submarine and its history is included in the price of admission. Call 415/929-0202.

MERCER CAVERNS

45-minute guided tours of the "Showplace of the Sierras." Beautiful and unusual crystalline formations, including stalactites, stalagmites, columns, curtains, flowstones and more.

Open Daily: Memorial Day through September 9 a.m.-5 p.m.; Saturday, Sunday and School Holidays: October through May 11 a.m. - 4 p.m.

One mile north of Murphy's, Calif., just off Hwy. 4. Call 209/728-2101.

Lake Tahoe's Finest Sightseeing

Enjoy a cruise on Lake Tahoe's original paddlewheeler, the M.S. Dixie, or discover the winter beauty of the "Top of Tahoe" with Zephyr Cove Snowmobile Center. Spectacular sightseeing and unbeatable hospitality--YEAR-ROUND!

Located 4 miles north of South Shore casinos on Hwy 50, Zephyr Cove, Nevada. Coupon must be presented at time of ticket purchase. Not valid with any other offer. Operated on lands of the USDA Forest Service.

The Mystery Spot

This unusual area is located in the midst of the redwood forest wherein visitors are shown numerous variations of gravity, perspective, compass, velocity and height during a 35-minute guided tour.

Open every day (9:30 a.m. to 5 p.m.); located at 1953 Branciforte Drive in Santa Cruz, California. For more information, brochure and directions, call (408) 423-8897 or write: The Mystery Spot, P.O. Box 2817, Santa Cruz, CA 95063.

RED & WHITE FLEET
A Crowley Company

Golden Gate Bay Cruise

$2.00 OFF Per Person

Good for up to six adults. Cannot be used with any other discount offer.

For Departure Time & Information : **(415) 546-BOAT**
BP

Ripley's
Believe It or Not!®

$1.50 off Regular Adult Admission
75¢ off Regular Child Admission

Maximum 6 per coupon. Not good with other discount offers. Expires 12/31/93.

Rosicrucian
Egyptian Museum
50% off
each adult admission

Maximum 8 adults per coupon. Cannot be used in conjunction with any other discount offer. Not for resale. Expires 12/31/93.

GOLDEN GATE BAY CRUISE

See the BEST of everything from the deck of a Red & White Fleet cruise boat. Depart from Fisherman's Wharf on this 45-minute tour that will cruise under the Golden Gate Bridge, by Sausalito in Marin County, past Angel Island and around Alcatraz. Listen to the history of San Francisco and the Golden Gate National Recreation Area, with first hand interviews that bring the sights to life before your eyes. Fully narrated in 4 languages: English, German, Japanese and Spanish.

Ripley's Believe It or Not! Museum

Experience the *odd*, the *unusual*...Two Floors, 11 Galleries, Actual Exhibits, State of the Art Displays and Illusions!
Sun.-Thurs. 10 AM-10PM; Fri./Sat. 10AM-Midnight. In the heart of Fisherman's Wharf on Jefferson near Taylor Street. Call 415/202-9850 or 202-9851.

Rosicrucian Egyptian Museum

Largest display of authentic ancient Egyptian and Mesopotamian artifacts in the Western United States. Open 9 to 5 seven days a week.

1600 block Park Ave.; Take I-80 to San Jose; Exit THE ALAMEDA 4 blocks south to Naglee Avenue and West 3 blocks to Park Avenue. For more information, call 408/287-2807.

THE SAN FRANCISCO
EXPERIENCE

"Feel the earth shake"

$2 off Adult Ticket

Maximum 2 per coupon. Not good with any other offers. Expires 12/31/93.

DOWN BY THE SEA STORE
at the **Santa Cruz Beach Boardwalk**

20% OFF ALL MERCHANDISE*

*20% off any purchase of $10 or more in the store, located near the Boardwalk's Haunted Castle at Walkway 4. Not for resale; one coupon per purchase. Expires December 31, 1993.

FAMILY FUN CENTER

Two-for-One Miniature Golf
Open 10 AM daily.
Not good with any other discounts or promotions.

The San Francisco Experience
Multi-Media Theatre

NOW SHOWING AT PIER 39 EVERY 1/2 HOUR EVERY DAY. An amazing wide screen production--35 projectors, wrap around sound, special effects. Feel the 1906 and 1989 earthquakes. Celebrate the Chinese New Year. Watch the fog roll in. And much more. Experience San Francisco in 30 thrilling minutes. There is nothing else like it. Call 415/982-7550.

SANTA CRUZ BEACH BOARDWALK

California's oldest amusement park provides old-fashioned family fun year round. Rides open daily Memorial Day to Labor Day and weekends throughout the year. Neptune's Kingdom adventure center and other attractions open daily except Dec. 25.
Take Highway 1 or 17 to Santa Cruz; follow signs to Main Beach/Boardwalk, 400 Beach Street, Santa Cruz, CA 95060. Call (408) 426-7433 for more information.

Scandia Family Fun Center

Featuring two award-winning miniature golf courses; L'il Indy Racers; Copenhagen Express miniature train; Batting Cages; Waterbugs and a Grand Arcade with more than 200 favorite video, pinball and skill games..
Suisun Valley Road exit off Interstate 80, 4300 Central Place, Suisun City, CA 94585.
Call 707/864-8338 (Park info); 707/864-8558 (Reservations); 707/864-8212 (Birthday information).

WORLD'S MOST COMPLETE
ANTIQUE FORD COLLECTION
$1 off adult admission with this coupon
Maximum 4 people per coupon.

Save $1.00 Per Person
(Good for up to 6 Guests)

Present this coupon at time of ticket purchase and receive a $1.00 discount on the Adult and Child Winchester Estate Tour. Coupons are not valid for organized groups, with any other discount offer, or for Night Tours. Coupon must be presented at time of ticket purchase.

24-Hour Information: 408/247-2101 Located on Winchester Blvd., Between Stevens Creek Blvd. & I-280.

101 Affordable Excursions

50% (Maze only) Validation No. 2329

Limit 4 Maze Tickets Per Coupon

Not valid with any other promotion.

500 Orange Dr. • Vacaville • (707) 446-3939
Between S.F. and Sacramento on I-80 and I-505
Call for Winter hours and rates

Index

The Perfect Gift

San Francisco and Beyond: 101 Affordable Excursions is the perfect gift for anyone living in or visiting northern California. Your friends and family will have fun with it year-round and enjoy it as a keepsake of their excursions. Show your appreciation for co-workers, volunteers, clients or teachers with a copy. If you borrowed this book, reward yourself with "the guidebook that makes fun free!"

Mail this order form to: Travel for Less Press
209 Apollo Dr., Suite 5
Hercules, CA 94547

San Francisco and Beyond:
101 Affordable Excursions @ $9.95 each   = _____

Sales Tax: Calif. residents add $.82 per book   = _____

Postage, handling & packaging:
Add $2.50 per book ($7.50 maximum)   = _____

Total = _____

Please include a check or money order payable to Travel for Less Press.

Your name: _____

Your telephone #: _____

Ship to name and address:_____

_____

City,State,Zip: _____

Call (510) 741-8440 for phone orders
or for information on quantity discounts.

About the Author

Pamela P. Hegarty has published more than 200 northern California travel articles. She writes for Good Housekeeping, Woman's Day, McCall's, San Francisco Focus, California Highways, Tours & Resorts, Golden State and Country Inns. She contributes to seven Fodor's guidebooks, including California and others focusing on the west. She is known in the East Bay as the Weekend Wanderer, a weekly columnist for the Contra Costa Times. Her stories also have appeared in the The San Jose Mercury News, Santa Rosa Press Democrat, Stockton Record, Boston Herald, New York Newsday, The San Francisco Examiner and more.